FOLLIES

FOLLIES

BOOK BY

JAMES GOLDMAN

MUSIC AND LYRICS BY

STEPHEN SONDHEIM

THEATRE COMMUNICATIONS GROUP
NEW YORK

Follies is published by Theatre Communications Group, Inc.,
520 Eighth Avenue, 24th Floor, New York, NY 10018–4156.

This publication is made possible in part with public funds from
the New York State Council on the Arts, a State Agency.

TCG books are exclusively distributed to the book trade by Consortium
Book Sales and Distribution.

LIBRARY OF CONGRESS CATALOGING-IN-PUBLICATION DATA

Sondheim, Stephen
[Follies. Libretto]
Follies / by Stephen Sondheim and James Goldman.— 1st ed.
p. cm.
ISBN 978-1-55936-417-1
1. Musicals—Librettos. I. Goldman, James. II. Title.
ML50.S705 F65 2001
782.1'4'0268—dc21   00-068276

Text design and composition by Lisa Govan

First TCG Edition, November 2001
New Edition, August 2011

Production History

Follies was originally presented on April 4, 1971, by Harold Prince in association with Ruth Mitchell at the Winter Garden Theatre in New York City. It was directed by Harold Prince and Michael Bennett. Scenic production was by Boris Aronson, with costumes by Florence Klotz, lighting by Tharon Musser, choreography by Michael Bennett, orchestrations by Jonathan Tunick, musical direction by Harold Hastings and dance music arrangements by John Berkman. The cast was as follows:

MAJORDOMO	Dick Laressa
SALLY DURANT PLUMMER	Dorothy Collins
YOUNG SALLY	Marti Rolph
CHRISTINE DONOVAN	Ethel Barrymore Colt
WILLY WHEELER	Fred Kelly
STELLA DEEMS	Mary McCarty
MAX DEEMS	John J. Martin
HEIDI SCHILLER	Justine Johnston
CHAUFFEUR	John Grigas
MEREDITH LANE	Sheila Smith
ROSCOE	Michael Bartlett
DEEDEE WEST	Helen Blount
HATTIE WALKER	Ethel Shutta
EMILY WHITMAN	Marcie Stringer
THEODORE WHITMAN	Charles Welch
VINCENT	Victor Griffin
VANESSA	Jayne Turner

YOUNG VINCENT	Michael Misita
YOUNG VANESSA	Graciela Daniele
SOLANGE LAFITTE	Fifi D'Orsay
CARLOTTA CAMPION	Yvonne De Carlo
PHYLLIS ROGERS STONE	Alexis Smith
BENJAMIN STONE	John McMartin
YOUNG PHYLLIS	Virginia Sandifur
YOUNG BEN	Kurt Peterson
BUDDY PLUMMER	Gene Nelson
YOUNG BUDDY	Harvey Evans
DIMITRI WEISMANN	Arnold Moss
YOUNG STELLA	Julie Pars
YOUNG HEIDI	Victoria Mallory
KEVIN	Ralph Nelson
PARTY MUSICIANS	Taft Jordan, Aaron Bell, Charles Spics, Robert Curtis
SHOWGIRLS	Suzanne Briggs, Trudy Carson, Kathie Dalton, Ursula Maschmeyer, Linda Perkins, Margot Travers
SINGERS AND DANCERS	Graciela Daniele, Mary Jane Houdina, Sonja Lekova, Rita O'Connor, Julie Pars, Suzanne Rogers, Roy Barry, Steve Boockvor, Michael Misita, Joseph Nelson, Ralph Nelson, Ken Urmston, Donald Weissmuller

The singers and dancers appeared as guests, waiters, waitresses, photographers, chorus girls, chorus boys, etc.

Follies opened on July 21, 1987, at the Shaftesbury Theatre, London. It was produced by Cameron Mackintosh and directed by Mike Ockrent. It was designed by Maria Björnson with lighting design by Mark Henderson, sound design by Andrew Bruce, choreography by Bob Avian, orchestrations by Jonathan Tunick, musical direction by Martin Koch and dance music arrangements by Chris Walker. The cast was as follows:

STAGE MANAGER	Roy Sone
RONNIE COHEN	Ronnie Price
DIMITRI WEISMANN	Leonard Sachs
CARLOTTA CAMPION	Dolores Gray
STELLA DEEMS	Lynda Baron
HEIDI SCHILLER	Adele Leigh
SOLANGE LAFITTE	Maria Charles
HATTIE WALKER	Margaret Courtenay
BILLIE WHITMAN	Pearl Carr
WALLY WHITMAN	Teddy Johnson
SALLY DURANT PLUMMER	Julia McKenzie
BUDDY PLUMMER	David Healy
PHYLLIS ROGERS STONE	Diana Rigg
BEN STONE	Daniel Massey
ROSCOE	Paul Bentley
YOUNG PHYLLIS	Gillian Bevan
YOUNG SALLY	Deborah Poplett
YOUNG BEN	Simon Green
YOUNG BUDDY	Evan Pappas
CHRISTINE DONOVAN	Josephine Gordon

DEEDEE WEST	Dorothy Vernon
MEREDITH LANE	Jill Martin
MAX BLANCK	Bruce Graham
YOUNG HEIDI	Michelle Todd
MARGIE	Sally Ann Triplett
PARTY GUESTS, WAITERS, FOLLIES BOYS AND STAGEHANDS	Luke Baxter, Peppi Borza, Brad Graham, Stephen Lübmann, Raymond Marlowe, Roy Sone, Roger Sutton, Julian Wild
THE FOLLIES GIRLS	Lisa Henson, Margaret Houston, Vanessa Leagh Hicks, Jennifer Scott Malden, Siobhan O'Kane, Dawn Spence, Catherine Terry

Follies opened on April 5, 2001, at New York City's Roundabout Theatre Company (Todd Haimes, Artistic Director; Ellen Richard, Managing Director). It was directed by Matthew Warchus. Set design was by Mark Thompson, with costume design by Theoni V. Aldrege, lighting design by Hugh Vanstone, sound design by Jonathan Deans, choreography by Kathleen Marshall, orchestrations by Jonathan Tunick, musical direction by Eric Stern with John Miller and dance music arrangements by John Berkman and David Chase. The cast was as follows:

DIMITRI WEISMANN	Louis Zorich
SALLY DURANT PLUMMER	Judith Ivey
PHYLLIS ROGERS STONE	Blythe Danner
BENJAMIN STONE	Gregory Harrison
BUDDY PLUMMER	Treat Williams
ROSCOE	Larry Raiken
DEEDEE WEST	Dorothy Stanley
HATTIE WALKER	Betty Garrett
SOLANGE LAFITTE	Jane White
EMILY WHITMAN	Marge Champion
THEODORE WHITMAN	Donald Saddler
SANDRA CRANE	Nancy Ringham
STELLA DEEMS	Carol Woods
SAM DEEMS	Peter Cormican
CARLOTTA CAMPION	Polly Bergen
HEIDI SCHILLER	Joan Roberts
YOUNG SALLY	Lauren Ward
YOUNG PHYLLIS	Erin Dilly

YOUNG BUDDY	Joey Sorge
YOUNG BEN	Richard Roland
YOUNG HEIDI	Brooke Sunny Moriber
YOUNG DEEDEE	Roxane Barlow
YOUNG EMILY	Carole Bentley
YOUNG CARLOTTA	Sally Mae Dunn
YOUNG SANDRA	Dottie Earle
YOUNG SOLANGE	Jacqueline Hendy
YOUNG HATTIE	Kelli O'Hara
YOUNG STELLA	Allyson Tucker
YOUNG THEODORE	Rod McCune
KEVIN	Stephen Campanella
BUDDY'S BLUES GIRLS	Roxane Barlow,
("Margie," "Sally")	Jessica Leigh Brown
SHOWGIRLS	Jessica Leigh Brown, Colleen Dunn,
	Amy Heggins, Wendy Waring
ENSEMBLE	Roxane Barlow, Carole Bentley,
	Jessica Leigh Brown, Stephen Campanella,
	Colleen Dunn, Sally Mae Dunn, Dottie Earle,
	Aldrin Gonzalez, Amy Heggins, Jacqueline Hendy,
	Rod McCune, Kelli O'Hara, T. Oliver Reid,
	Alex Sanchez, Allyson Tucker, Matt Wall,
	Wendy Waring

A new full-scale production of *Follies* opened on May 21, 2001, at The John F. Kennedy Center for the Performing Arts (David M. Rubenstein, Chairman; Michael M. Kaiser, President; Max A. Woodward, Vice President) in Washington, D.C. This production (with some cast changes) transferred and opened on Broadway on September 12, 2011, at the Marquis Theatre. It was produced there by The John F. Kennedy Center for the Performing Arts; Nederlander Presentations, Inc.; Adrienne Arsht; HRH Foundation; and Allan Williams (Executive Producer). It was directed by Eric Schaeffer. The choreography was by Warren Carlyle, set design by Derek McLane, costume design by Gregg Barnes, lighting design by Natasha Katz and sound design by Kai Harada. The music director was James Moore and orchestrations were by Jonathan Tunick. Additionally, at the Marquis, the dance music arranger was John Berkman and the music coordinator was John Miller. The production stage managers were Shari Silberglitt (Kennedy Center) and Arthur Gaffin (Marquis). The cast was as follows:

SALLY DURANT PLUMMER	Bernadette Peters
YOUNG SALLY	Lora Lee Gayer
SANDRA CRANE	Florence Lacey
YOUNG SANDRA	Kiira Schmidt
DEEDEE WEST	Colleen Fitzpatrick
YOUNG DEEDEE	Leslie Donna Flesner
SOLANGE LAFITTE	Régine (KC) / Mary Beth Peil (M)
YOUNG SOLANGE	Ashley Yeater
HATTIE WALKER	Linda Lavin (KC) / Jayne Houdyshell (M)

YOUNG HATTIE	Jenifer Foote
ROSCOE	Michael Hayes
STELLA DEEMS	Terri White
YOUNG STELLA	Erin N. Moore
MAX DEEMS	Frederick Strother
HEIDI SCHILLER	Rosalind Elias
YOUNG HEIDI	Leah Horowitz
EMILY WHITMAN	Susan Watson
YOUNG EMILY	Danielle Jordan
THEODORE WHITMAN	Terrence Currier (KC) / Don Correia (M)
CARLOTTA CAMPION	Elaine Paige
YOUNG CARLOTTA	Pamela Otterson
PHYLLIS ROGERS STONE	Jan Maxwell
YOUNG PHYLLIS	Kirsten Scott
BENJAMIN STONE	Ron Raines
YOUNG BEN	Nick Vernia
BUDDY PLUMMER	Danny Burstein
YOUNG BUDDY	Christian Delcroix
DIMITRI WEISMANN	David Sabin
KEVIN	Clifton Samuels
BUDDY'S BLUES "MARGIE"	Kiira Schmidt
BUDDY'S BLUES "SALLY"	Jenifer Foote
ENSEMBLE	Lawrence Alexander, Brandon Bieber, John Carroll, Leslie Donna Flesner, Jenifer Foote, Leah Horowitz, Suzanne Hylenski, Danielle Jordan, Amanda Kloots-Larsen, Brittany Marcin, Erin N. Moore, Pamela Otterson, Clifton Samuels, Kiira Schmidt, Brian Shepard, Sam Strasfeld, Ashley Yeater (all KC and M); Amos Wolff (M)
SWINGS	Sara Edwards (KC and M), Amos Wolff (KC), Matthew deGuzman (M)

CHARACTERS

Dimitri Weismann

"The Weismann Girls"
Sally Durant Plummer
Young Sally
Phyllis Rogers Stone
Young Phyllis
Carlotta Campion
Young Carlotta
Hattie Walker
Young Hattie
Stella Deems
Young Stella
Solange LaFitte
Young Solange
Heidi Schiller
Young Heidi
Emily Whitman
Young Emily
Sandra Crane
Young Sandra
Deedee West
Young Deedee

Benjamin Stone
Young Ben
Buddy Plummer
Young Buddy
Roscoe
Sam Deems
Young Theodore
Kevin, a waiter
Ladies and Gentlemen
    of the Ensemble

SCENE

A party on the stage of the Weismann Theatre

TIME

Tonight

MUSICAL NUMBERS

Beautiful Girls	*Roscoe and Company*
Don't Look at Me	*Sally and Ben*
Waiting for the Girls Upstairs	*Buddy, Ben, Phyllis, Sally, Young Buddy, Young Ben, Young Phyllis and Young Sally*
Rain on the Roof	*The Whitmans*
Ah, Paris!	*Solange*
Broadway Baby	*Hattie*
The Road You Didn't Take	*Ben*
Bolero d'Amour	*Danced by Vincent and Vanessa*
In Buddy's Eyes	*Sally*
Who's That Woman?	*Stella and Company*
I'm Still Here	*Carlotta*
Too Many Mornings	*Ben and Sally*
The Right Girl	*Buddy*
One More Kiss	*Heidi and Young Heidi*
Could I Leave You?	*Phyllis*

Loveland

THE FOLLY OF LOVE

Loveland	*Company*

THE FOLLY OF YOUTH

You're Gonna Love Tomorrow/Love Will See Us Through	*Young Ben and Young Phyllis Young Buddy and Young Sally*

BUDDY'S FOLLY

The God-Why-Don't-You-Love-Me Blues	*Buddy, "Margie" and "Sally"*

SALLY'S FOLLY

Losing My Mind	*Sally*

PHYLLIS'S FOLLY

The Story of Lucy and Jessie	*Phyllis and Company*

BEN'S FOLLY

Live, Laugh, Love	*Ben and Company*

ACT I

The theatre curtain is an old asbestos fire curtain, covered with dust, unused for years. There is the sound of soft tympani, like thunder from a long time ago. Slowly the curtain starts to rise.

Music begins; soft, slow, strange. The stage is dark and mysterious. Standing center is the one and only Dimitri Weismann, flashlight in hand, surveying the remnants of his once famous theatre.

From the shadows behind him he hears the eerie sound of footsteps hurrying along the metal gantry. He swings his flashlight up into the darkness; nothing there. Silence. Then from the dark auditorium rises the ghostly sound of audience applause. The applause fades; silence again.

Now the muffled sound of an argument coming from above the auditorium ceiling; then the sound of a slamming door. Weismann shines the flashlight into the depths of the stage, walks toward a metal staircase at the back wall and starts to climb it.

The music swells to a climax when suddenly revealed on the gantry center stage is a Showgirl. She stands motionless. She is tall, slim and beautiful. She is unseen by Weismann as he passes her and exits through a dressing-room door.

Slowly she comes to life, as if she were a ghost who had been waiting in the theatre for years in anticipation. She moves as showgirls did—but slower, almost drifting. From darkness, out of nowhere, comes another Showgirl, like the first, then another.

Then the heavy door upstage right slides open and a shaft of light spills onto the stage, revealing a lone figure tentatively entering the old theatre. It is Sally Durant Plummer. She is blond, petite, sweet-faced and, at forty-nine, still remarkably like the girl she was thirty years ago.

SALLY *(To Weismann's Assistant silhouetted at the entrance)*: Thank you, that's so sweet. I know I'm early, I wanted to be first.

(The ghostly Showgirls, unseen by Sally, gaze on the new arrival with strange curiosity.)

I just couldn't wait. I haven't seen New York in thirty years and all my friends.

(Weismann's Assistant stays silhouetted in the doorway as Sally moves downstage.)

I'm Sally Durant Plummer. You can't imagine how glamorous it was or what it meant to be a Weismann Girl. The way it felt to come onstage, all those eyes looking at you . . . It's going to be a lovely party. I'm so glad I came.

(As the ghostly Showgirls move inquisitively toward Sally, the slow, strange music swells, strikes an expectant chord and cuts to bright, light-hearted pastiche tunes of the 1920s and 1930s as . . .

The guests arrive. The stage is suddenly filled with color and energy, as couple after couple, ranging in age from their fifties to their eighties, move about excitedly.

In the midst of the excitement, Ben Stone and Phyllis Rogers Stone enter. Phyllis is a tall and queenly woman, stylish and intelligent. Her fine-boned face is probably more beautiful now than it was thirty years ago. Her husband Ben is tall, trim, distinguished; a successful and authoritative man.

They move downstage, wryly taking in the scene.

PHYLLIS: Lord, will you look at it.

BEN: Another theatre comes down. What kind of loving wife are you to drag me here?

PHYLLIS: I wanted to come back, Ben. One last look at where it all began. I wanted something when I came here thirty years ago but I forgot to write it down and God knows what it was.

BEN: Well, I'm glad you're glad to be here: that makes one of us.

PHYLLIS: Oh Ben, I love the way you hate it when I'm happy and you're not.

(She turns, mingles with the other guests. More guests arrive, among them Buddy Plummer. In his early fifties, he's appealing, lively, outgoing and, like the other principals, he is dealing with a lot of thoughts and feelings he can't express.)

BUDDY *(Smiling to a guest)*: My wife . . . she took the early plane. You haven't seen her, have you? Blond, cute as hell, about so high.

(The guest shakes his head. Buddy, still smiling, turns to another guest.)

It's crazy—all the traveling I do, I can't get used to flying. Once I met this fellow out in Denver—Salt Lake City. Anyway, he's in the airport bar and is he stoned. He's scared of planes, he tells me, so I say, "Look, fella, if it's that bad, miss the flight." "I can't," the guy says, "I'm the pilot."

(Buddy laughs, shoulder-slapping the other guests. The music rises. There is sudden excitement. Standing in a spotlight, motionless, is Dimitri Weismann. Now we can see him clearly. He is an acerbic, charming, energetic man. He must be eighty, but looks no more than sixty-five.)

WEISMANN: So many of you came. Amazing. Welcome to our first—and last—reunion. It's 1971; time marches on. Though I've aged in thirty years, let me assure you I am still Dimitri Weismann. Every year between the Great Wars, I produced a Follies in this theatre. Since then, this house has been a home to ballet, rep, movies, blue movies and, now, in a final burst of glory, it's to be a parking lot. Before it goes, I felt an urge to see you one last time . . . a final chance to glamorize the old days, stumble through a song or two and lie about ourselves a little. I have, as you can see, spared no expense. Still, there's a band, free food and drink, and the inevitable Roscoe, here as always to bring on the Weismann Girls. So take one last look at your girls. They won't be coming down these stairs again. Maestro, if you please!

(All the former Follies girls move to the wings, the band starts to vamp and Roscoe, an elderly tenor in top hat, white tie and tails, appears high on a stairway. He strikes a majestic pose, and in an absolutely glorious voice begins to sing:)

ROSCOE:
> Hats off,
> Here they come, those
> Beautiful girls.
> That's what
> You've been waiting for.
>
> Nature never fashioned
> A flower so fair.

No rose can compare—
Nothing respectable
Half so delectable.

Cheer them
In their glory,
Diamonds and pearls,
Dazzling jewels
By the score.

This is what beauty can be,
Beauty celestial, the best, you'll agree:
All for you,
These beautiful girls!

(Roscoe steps back. The music soars up as the full orchestra takes over.

Spotlights strike Deedee West, posed as she was thirty years ago, about to make her grand entrance down the Follies stairs. She wears, all the women do, a sash on which her Follies year appears in gold. She smiles and starts down.

One by one, all the women follow. Some are grand and sure, some are flustered or self-conscious, some amused, some very serious. The years on their sashes range from 1918 to 1941, and it feels as if an entire era were coming down the stairs.

Once down, the women parade across the stage just as they did all those years before. As they move across the stage, everybody sings:)

ALL:

Careful,
Here's the home of
Beautiful girls,
Where your
Reason is undone.

Beauty
Can't be hindered
From taking its toll.
You may lose control.
Faced with these Loreleis,
What man can moralize?

Caution,
On your guard with
Beautiful girls,
Flawless charmers every one.
This is how Samson was shorn:
Each in her style a Delilah reborn,
Each a gem,
A beautiful diadem
Of beautiful—welcome them—

ROSCOE:
These beautiful—

ALL:
Girls!

(The line of women across the stage breaks up the instant the singing ends. There are shouted greetings and squeals, hugs and kisses. Waiters move about with trays of drinks. Sally, dazzled by the wonder of it all, is standing, smiling, taking it all in. She doesn't see Buddy until he comes up to her.)

BUDDY: Hi honey.
SALLY: Oh Buddy, you did come. Did I look all right?
BUDDY: Like you're twenty-one again. I mean it. Just look at you. How was your flight? You watch the movie?
SALLY: Don't be angry with me Buddy. I had to be here.
BUDDY: It's okay; we'll work it out.
SALLY: I wanted to so much.

BUDDY: I know, I know you did . . .
SALLY: Oh, look; there's Stella Deems. I've got to talk to her.

(Sally heads toward Stella as Buddy drifts into the party. Hattie Walker approaches Ben, autograph book in hand. Phyllis joins them.)

HATTIE *(Shows the autograph book to Ben)*: Mr. Stone, would you mind? For my grandson.
BEN: Nonsense, I'd be delighted. What's your grandson's name?
HATTIE: Jerome. He's eleven, but he reads all your speeches.
BEN: A misspent youth. I spent mine in the local music hall. It had a broken fire door and I saw every show that came to town. You wore a white dress cut to here. I didn't hear a note you sang. *(Handing book back)* Next time you find him reading, send him out to look for broken doors.
HATTIE: Mr. Stone, you sure know how to make a girl feel good.

(Hattie walks away.)

PHYLLIS: My God, you're charming.
BEN: You should see me when you're not around.
PHYLLIS *(Referring to Solange LaFitte, who is dressed outrageously, talking energetically to Weismann)*: They might have told us it was a costume party.
SOLANGE: Mitya, mon cher, it's me—Solange LaFitte. You know what I've been doing since my style went out of style? I sell more perfume than Chanel. *(Takes bottle from her evening bag)* "Caveman" by Solange. For men who have an air about them. Vulgar, but my darling, it will change your life. *(Posing)* I ask you, is it possible to look like this at sixty-nine?
WEISMANN: It must be magic.
SOLANGE *(Taking out another bottle)*: "Magic" by Solange.

(She strolls away with Weismann as we find Emily and Theodore Whitman in animated conversation with Sandra Crane.)

THEODORE: We bought an Arthur Murray franchise.
EMILY: Smartest thing we ever did.
THEODORE: We teach dance for a living.

(They do a nifty dance step.)

EMILY: We're still a team.

(They dance away as Sally moves in with Stella and Sam Deems.)

STELLA: . . . We had a hard time letting go. We kept on working all through '42. Then one day—we were doing daytime radio in Philly—and Sam, he turned to me and said, "Stella, baby, this is a load of crap." The mike was open. Fifty thousand housewives heard the news.
SAM: The next day, we were on the way to Florida. She helps me in the store.
STELLA: I do all my singing in the tub. It's the cat's pajamas. Great seeing you again . . .
SALLY: Sally.
STELLA: Right.

(Sally turns to face the audience and sings softly:)

SALLY:
> Ta-da!
> Now, folks, we bring you,
> Di-rect from Phoenix,
> Live and in person,
> Sally Durant!
> Here she is at last,
> Twinkle in her eye—

PHYLLIS: Sally?

(Young Phyllis and Young Sally enter, unseen by Phyllis and Sally.)

YOUNG PHYLLIS: Sally! Sally, come on, will you? That's our call.
YOUNG SALLY: Oh God, my hook's undone.
YOUNG PHYLLIS: Let me.
YOUNG SALLY: Okay, okay.

(They giggle and throw their arms around each other.)

PHYLLIS: Sally . . . it is you, isn't it?
SALLY: Phyllis! You came, you're here. Just look at you. I want to hug you, but I can't. You're like a queen or something.
PHYLLIS: Well, if you can't, I can.

(They embrace as Young Phyllis and Young Sally break apart.)

YOUNG PHYLLIS: Hurry, hurry.

(Young Phyllis and Young Sally exit.)

PHYLLIS: Sally, you look just as cute as ever.
SALLY: Me? I've got a tummy and my hair's too dyed. Who cares? New York's all changed. This afternoon when I walked past 44th and Third—why, Phyl, it wasn't there.
PHYLLIS: What wasn't?
SALLY: Our apartment, where we lived. Don't you remember? Five flights up. I did the cleaning and you cooked: baked beans and peanut butter sandwiches.
PHYLLIS: You never made the beds.
SALLY: I still don't, sometimes. And that awful bathtub in the kitchen . . .
PHYLLIS: You know, I think I loved it.
SALLY: You were homesick and you cried a lot, but we had fun.

PHYLLIS: You married Buddy, didn't you?

SALLY *(Nodding)*: You married Ben. I know. I read about you in the magazines. I even saw your living room in *Vogue*. It's all white. Is Ben still in Washington?

PHYLLIS: He's out of politics. He's president of a foundation now. Here in New York.

SALLY: He's here now? Here tonight?

PHYLLIS: Yes, he'll be so happy to see you.

(They go off into the crowd. Elsewhere in the party, Buddy spies Ben.)

BUDDY: Well, whaddaya know? Hey, Ben. Ben Stone.

BEN: Buddy.

BUDDY: You look great.

BEN: Don't let appearances deceive you.

(They hug.)

BUDDY: Not a chance. I've missed you, Ben.

BEN: You know how many years it's been.

BUDDY: Don't count. I wasn't sure you'd come.

BEN: Blame Phyllis.

(Young Ben and Young Buddy enter, Ben and Buddy can't see them.)

YOUNG BUDDY: I got you a terrific date tonight.

YOUNG BEN: I can't, Buddy. I've got to study.

YOUNG BUDDY: Aw, come on, Ben. It's all fixed up. She's Sally's roommate.

YOUNG BEN: I don't know.

YOUNG BUDDY: Her name is Phyllis something.

YOUNG BEN: What's she like?

YOUNG BUDDY: Nice girl. She's lonely. Do the kid a favor. Whatcha got to lose?

(Young Ben and Young Buddy fade away.)

BUDDY: I always knew you'd make it big.

BEN: I've had a lot of luck.

BUDDY: Me, too. I mean, you grow up hearing it's the little things that count, turns out it's true. I come home from a trip, see Sally, and I'm glad to see her. No big deal, no fireworks. I'm sentimental on my second drink. You ever play around?

BEN: I gave all that up years ago.

BUDDY: Same here. Not like the old days, is it? Law school, who could study? I'd have made some lousy lawyer. No regrets; right, Ben?

(Carlotta Campion enters and calls to Ben:)

CARLOTTA: Ben Stone!

BEN: No regrets.

(Ben turns to Carlotta as Buddy drifts off into the party.)

BEN: Well, it's not much of a ball to be the belle of, but congratulations anyway. That outfit is a triumph of restraint.

CARLOTTA: I always liked the way you talk. I haven't seen your picture in the papers lately.

BEN: Thanks, the same to you.

CARLOTTA: You ought to watch more television. I've got a series of my own.

SALLY *(Watching from a distance)*: Ben?

(Young Sally enters as Carlotta goes back to the party.)

YOUNG SALLY: Ben. Ben Stone, I want a reason. Look at me, damn it. You turn around and look at me!

SALLY *(Quietly)*: Ben, it's me.

11

(The memory fades as Sally, working up her courage to confront Ben, starts to sing:)

>Now, folks, we bring you,
>Di-rect from Phoenix,
>Live and in person,
>Sally Durant!
>Here she is at last,
>Twinkle in her eye,
>Hot off the press,
>Strictly a mess,
>Nevertheless . . .

(Smiling nervously.)

Hi, Ben.

(Then, before he can respond:)

>No, don't look at me—
>Please, not just yet.
>Why am I here? This is crazy!
>No, don't look at me—
>I know that face,
>You're trying to place
>The name . . .
>Say something, Ben, anything.

>No, don't talk to me.
>Ben, I forget:
>What were we like, it's so hazy!
>Look at these people,
>Aren't they eerie?
>Look at this party,
>Isn't it dreary?
>I'm so glad I came.

(Music continues under the following:)

BEN *(Looking at her)*: Can I look now?

(She nods, smiling nervously.)

Yes, it's possible. You might be Sally. Did you fall asleep at Toscanini broadcasts? *(She nods)* Did you eat Baby Ruths for breakfast?

SALLY: I still do sometimes. Oh, Ben, you're just the way I knew you'd be. You make me feel like I was nineteen and the four of us were going on the town.

SALLY AND BEN *(Singing)*:
>So—
>Just look at us . . .

SALLY:
>Fat . . .

BEN:
>Turning gray . . .

SALLY AND BEN:
>Still playing games,
>Acting crazy.

SALLY:
>Isn't it awful?

BEN:
>God, how depressing—

SALLY AND BEN:
>Me, I'm a hundred,
>You, you're a blessing—
>I'm so glad I came!

BEN: What we need is a drink.

(The music ends. Sally and Ben walk off together. A spotlight comes up on Carlotta, deep in conversation with Sandra. The orchestra begins to play "One More Kiss.")

CARLOTTA: I never get to talk. I take a plane, go to a party, every guy I meet says, "Boy, oh boy, a real live movie actress; tell me all about yourself." I get as far as: "I was born in Idaho," and he starts telling me the story of *his* life. Not just his troubles: he unloads the whole thing, ups and downs. Mostly, he just wants to talk. Sometimes, he wants a place to put his head a while. Other times, he wants the works: some nights, he gets it.

(Focus shifts to Hattie and Deedee.)

HATTIE: . . . Yes, yes, I know. It's always sad to lose a husband. I've lost five. You wouldn't think it now, to look at me. I've always married crazy boys. They raced around in motor cars and aeroplanes. They lived too fast, but while they lived, my goodness, it was something.

(Heidi Schiller enters alone, listening to the strains of "One More Kiss." On a platform above her, Young Heidi appears. For a moment Heidi and Young Heidi are both listening to the music.
Weismann enters.)

HEIDI: Mitya, listen. That's my waltz they're playing. You remember?
WEISMANN: Heidi, could I possibly forget?
HEIDI: Franz Lehar wrote it for me in Vienna. I was having coffee in my drawing room. In ran Franz and straight to the piano: "Liebchen, it's for you." Or was it Oscar Strauss? *(Pauses)* Facts never interest me. What matters is the song.

(They exit together. Focus shifts to Phyllis and Buddy.)

PHYLLIS: Oh, Buddy, no; I didn't really do that, did I?

BUDDY: Cross my heart. In Central Park. You and Sally both
dove in. We dared you to.

PHYLLIS: God, it's so good to see you—and what fun it was to
do things. Ben and I don't do things anymore—we say
them. Life is like a soundtrack, words with all the action
missing. Why, we've even got a chauffeur who's articulate.

BUDDY: Some life you've got. Me, I'm in oil these days. Sounds
big but it isn't. I'm a salesman and we sell these rigs and
drills. I'm good at selling. Takes me on the road a lot, but
I like meeting people, going places; keeps the juices flow-
ing. *(Pauses)* Phyl, look around you. Stage door, call
board. God, the time we clocked here, me and Ben. The
place was always packed with guys and flowers, waiting
for the girls to come down.

YOUNG BUDDY'S VOICE *(Sings)*:
    Hey, up there . . .

BUDDY: I even carved my name here some place.

YOUNG BUDDY'S VOICE *(Sings)*:
    Way up there . . .

YOUNG BUDDY AND YOUNG BEN'S VOICES *(Sing)*:
    Whaddaya say, up there?

BUDDY: Just being back together here, the four of us, I feel all
the things I used to feel. Like it was yesterday.

PHYLLIS: Oh, Buddy, that was 1941; that's thirty years ago.

(Ben and Sally join them.)

BEN: Corsages, Sally? Are you sure about that?

SALLY: Every night, you'd bring them.

BUDDY: Bought them from the lady on the corner.

PHYLLIS: Yesterday's gardenias.

SALLY: And then we'd go and dance all night at Tommy's.

BUDDY: Tony's.

BEN: Tony's. Well, my God.

(Buddy sings up to the flies:)

BUDDY:

> Hey, up there!
> Way up there!
> Whaddaya say, up there?

I see it all. It's like a movie in my head that plays and plays.
It isn't just the bad things I remember. It's the whole show.

> Waiting around for the girls upstairs
> After the curtain came down,
> Money in my pocket to spend.
> "Honey, could you maybe get a friend for my friend?"

BEN:

> Hearing the sound of the girls above
> Dressing to go on the town,

BUDDY:

> Clicking heels on steel and cement,

BEN:

> Picking up the giggles floating down through the vent,

BUDDY AND BEN:

> Goddamnedest hours that I ever spent
> Were waiting for the girls
> Upstairs.

BUDDY:

    Hey, up there!
    Way up there!
    Whaddaya say, up there?

BEN:

    That's where the keys hung and
    That's were you picked up your mail.

BUDDY:

    I remember:
    Me and Ben,
    Me and Ben,
    We'd come around at ten,
    Me and Ben,
    And hang around the wings
    Watching things
    With what-the-hell-was-his-name,
    You know, the old guy . . .
    Max! I remember . . .

    Anyway,
    There we'd stay
    Until the curtain fell.
    And when the curtain fell,
    Then all hell broke:
    Girls on the run
    And scenery flying,
    Doors slamming left and right.

BEN:

    Girls in their un-
    Dies, blushing but trying
    Not to duck out of sight.

BUDDY AND BEN:

> Girls by the hun-
> Dreds waving and crying,
> "See you tomorrow night!"
> Girls looking frazzled and girls looking great,
> Girls in a frenzy to get a date,
> Girls like a madhouse and two of them late . . .
> And who had to wait?
> And wait . . .
> And wait . . .
> And . . .

PHYLLIS:

> Waiting around for the boys downstairs,
> Stalling as long as we dare.
> Which dress from my wardrobe of two?
> One of them was borrowed and the other was blue.

SALLY:

> Holding our ground for the boys below,
> Fussing around with our hair,

PHYLLIS:

> Giggling, wriggling out of our tights.

SALLY:

> Chattering and clattering down all of those flights—

SALLY AND PHYLLIS:

> God, I'd forgotten there ever were nights
> Of waiting for the boys
> Downstairs.

BUDDY:

> You up there!

SALLY:

Down in a minute!

BEN:

You two up there!

PHYLLIS:

Just keep your shirts on!

BUDDY AND BEN:

Aren't you through up there?

SALLY AND PHYLLIS:

Heard you the first time!

(Young Buddy, Young Ben, Young Sally and Young Phyllis enter.)

BUDDY AND BEN,
   YOUNG BUDDY AND
   YOUNG BEN:

Look, are you coming or
Aren't you coming 'cause
Look, if we're going, we
Gotta get going 'cause
Look, they won't hold us
A table at ringside all
Night!

SALLY AND PHYLLIS,
   YOUNG SALLY AND
   YOUNG PHYLLIS:

Coming, we're coming, will
You hold your horses, we're
Coming, we're ready, be
There in a jiffy, we're
Coming, we're coming. All
Right!

YOUNG SALLY:

Hi . . .

YOUNG BEN:

Girls . . .

YOUNG PHYLLIS:

Ben . . .

YOUNG BUDDY:
    Sally . . .

YOUNG SALLY:
    Boy, we're beat.

YOUNG BUDDY:
    You look neat.

YOUNG PHYLLIS:
    We saw you in the wings.

YOUNG BEN:
    How are things?

YOUNG PHYLLIS:
    Did someone pass you in?

YOUNG BUDDY:
    Slipped a fin
    To what-the-hell-is-his-name,
    You know, the doorman.

YOUNG PHYLLIS:
    Al?

YOUNG BUDDY:
    No.

YOUNG SALLY:
    Big?

YOUNG BEN:
    Fat.

YOUNG PHYLLIS:
    Young?

YOUNG BUDDY:
Bald.

YOUNG SALLY:
Harry!

YOUNG BEN:
Yeah.

YOUNG SALLY:
Okey-doaks.

YOUNG BUDDY:
Come on, folks.

YOUNG PHYLLIS:
And where we gonna go?

YOUNG BEN:
A little joint I know—

YOUNG SALLY:
What?

YOUNG BUDDY:
Great new show there.

YOUNG PHYLLIS:
Hey, I thought you said tonight'd be Tony's—

YOUNG BUDDY:
This joint is just as grand.

YOUNG SALLY:
We girls got dressed for dancing at Tony's—

YOUNG BEN:
> This joint is in demand.

YOUNG SALLY AND YOUNG PHYLLIS:
> Ta-ta, good-bye, you'll find us at Tony's—

YOUNG BUDDY AND YOUNG BEN:
> Wait till you hear the band!

YOUNG SALLY AND YOUNG PHYLLIS:	YOUNG BUDDY AND YOUNG BEN:
You told us Tony's, That we'd go to Tony's.	I told you Tony's? I never said Tony's.

SALLY AND PHYLLIS, YOUNG SALLY AND YOUNG PHYLLIS:	BUDDY AND BEN, YOUNG BUDDY AND YOUNG BEN:
Then Ben mentioned Tony's.	

Well, someone said Tony's. There's dancing at Tony's— All right, then, we'll go!	When's Ben mentioned Tony's? It's ritzy at Tony's— All right, then, we'll go!

(And, as suddenly as they appeared, the memories are gone. Ben, Phyllis, Buddy and Sally stand quite still for a moment, caught by the remembered joy of being young. Then, as the music pulses on, they snap back to the present, look at one another, then away, all deeply shaken by the immediacy of the past and by regret for what's been lost and wasted. Angrily at first, they turn toward us and sing:)

BUDDY:
> Waiting around for the girls upstairs,
> Weren't we chuckleheads then?

BEN:
>Very young and very old hat—
>Everybody has to go through stages like that.

SALLY, PHYLLIS, BUDDY AND BEN:
>Waiting around for the girls upstairs—
>Thank you but never again.
>Life was fun but, oh, so intense.
>Everything was possible and nothing made sense
>Back there when one of the major events
>Was waiting for the girls,
>Waiting for the girls,
>Waiting for the girls,
>Upstairs.

(Blackout.

>*In the darkness we hear the sound of ghostly applause,
>gradually increasing in volume, as though the theatre were
>reawakening. Showgirl ghosts look on as the Whitmans,
>Solange and Hattie appear in separate pools of light. They
>relive their old Follies solos: "Rain on the Roof," "Ah,
>Paris!" and "Broadway Baby":)*

EMILY AND THEODORE:
>Listen to the rain on the roof go
>Pit-pitty-pat
>Pit-pitty-pat-pitty,
>Sit, kitty cat,
>We won't get home for hours.
>Relax and
>Listen to the rain on the roof go
>Plunk-planka-plink
>Plunk-planka-plink-planka,
>Let's have a drink
>And shelter from the showers.

Rain, rain, don't go away,
Fill up the sky.
Rain through the night,
We'll stay
Cozy and dry.

Listen to the rain on the roof go
Pit-pitty-pat
(They kiss)
Plunk-a-plink
(Kiss)
Plank
(Kiss)
Pity that
It's not a hurricane.
Listen—plink—to the
(Kiss, kiss)
Lovely rain.

SOLANGE:

New York has neon, Berlin has bars,
But ah! Paris! *(Pronounced "Paree!")*
Shanghai has silk and Madrid guitars,
But ah! Paris!
In Cairo you find bizarre bazaars,
In London: pip! pip! you sip tea.
But when it comes to love,
None of the above
Compares, *compris*?
So if it's making love
That you're thinking of,
Ah ah ah ah ah ah ah ah ah! Paris!

I have seen the ruins of Rome,
I've been in the igloos of Nome.
I have gone to Moscow, it's very gay—

Well, anyway,
On the first of May!
I have seen Rangoon and Soho,
And I like them more than so-so.
But when there's a moon,
Good-bye, Rangoon—
Hello, Montmartre, hello!

Peking has rickshaws, New Orleans jazz,
But ah! Paris!
Beirut has sunshine—that's all it has,
But ah! Paris!
Constantinople has Turkish baths *(Pronounced "bazz")*
And Athens that lovely debris.
Carlsbad may have a spa,
But for *ooh-la-la*,
You come with me!
Carlsbad is where you're cured
After you have toured
Ah ah ah ah ah ah ah ah ah! Paris!

HATTIE:

I'm just a
Broadway baby.
Walking off my tired feet.
Pounding Forty-second Street
To be in a show.
Broadway baby,
Learning how to sing and dance,
Waiting for that one big chance
To be in a show.

Gee,
I'd like to be
On some marquee,
All twinkling lights,

A spark
To pierce the dark
From Battery Park
Way up to Washington Heights.
Some day, maybe,
All my dreams will be repaid:
Heck, I'd even play the maid
To be in a show.

Say, Mr. Producer,
I'm talking to you, sir:
I don't need a lot,
Only what I got,
Plus a tube of greasepaint
And a follow-spot!

I'm just a Broadway baby,
Slaving at the five-and-ten,
Dreaming of the great day when
I'll be in a show.
Broadway baby,
Making rounds all afternoon,
Eating at a greasy spoon
To save on my dough.

At
My tiny flat
There's just my cat,
A bed and a chair.
Still
I'll stick it till
I'm on a bill
All over Times Square.

Some day maybe,
If I stick it long enough

I may get to strut my stuff
Working for a nice man
Like a Ziegfeld or a Weismann

HATTIE, SOLANGE, EMILY AND THEODORE:
In a great big
Broadway show!

(The memory is shattered by a noisy return of the party guests. A Photographer enters with Weismann. All the old Follies performers gather for a group photograph.)

PHOTOGRAPHER: All right, here we go: 5, 4, 3, 2, 1.

(The camera flashes, capturing the entire group in one extravagant, theatrical pose. There is a ghostly moment of silence. Then, as the group breaks up:)

WEISMANN: Are there any hungry actors in the house? Follow me.
EMILY WHITMAN: Mr. Weismann did not discover us. George M. Cohan beat him to it. Right, dear?
THEODORE WHITMAN: Right.
SOLANGE: Chevalier himself discovered me.
HATTIE: In bed, I'll bet.

(They drift off. The only two people left on stage are Ben and Sally.)

SALLY: Oh, Ben, your life must be so thrilling. All the famous people and the parties.
BEN: Oh, yes. The diplomats love telling dirty stories and the writers brag about their picture deals, and all the opera singers talk about is food.
SALLY: Honestly?
BEN: Would I lie to you? No, it's a good life really. After all, success is being good at doing what you want to do. Know what you want and do it, that's the secret.

(He sings:)

BEN:

You're either a poet
Or you're a lover
Or you're the famous
Benjamin Stone.
You take one road,
You try one door,
There isn't time for any more.
One's life consists of either/or.
One has regrets
Which one forgets,
And as the years go on,

The road you didn't take
Hardly comes to mind,
Does it?
The door you didn't try,
Where could it have led?
The choice you didn't make
Never was defined,
Was it?
Dreams you didn't dare
Are dead.
Were they ever there?
Who said?
I don't remember,
I don't remember
At all.

(Ben stops, stands still, remembering, as the music continues under and the lights reveal Young Ben and Young Buddy walking along. Young Ben is dressed up for a date.)

YOUNG BUDDY *(Handing a set of keys to Young Ben)*: Here you go. Keys to the old jalopy.

YOUNG BEN: Thanks.

YOUNG BUDDY *(Taking out his wallet)*: You need a couple of bucks?

YOUNG BEN: I'm fine.

YOUNG BUDDY: Come on, it's only money, what's it matter?

YOUNG BEN: You wouldn't know.

BEN:

> The books I'll never read
> Wouldn't change a thing,
> Would they?
> The girls I'll never know
> I'm too tired for.
> The lives I'll never lead
> Couldn't make me sing,
> Could they? Could they? Could they?
> Chances that you miss,
> Ignore.
> Ignorance is bliss—
> What's more,
> You won't remember,
> You won't remember
> At all,
> Not at all.

(Young Phyllis appears.)

YOUNG BEN: Borrowed money, borrowed car. Some day I'm going to have the biggest goddamn limousine.

YOUNG PHYLLIS: We've got each other, Ben. What difference does it make?

YOUNG BEN: All the difference.

BEN:
You yearn for the women,
Long for the money,
Envy the famous
Benjamin Stones.
You take your road,   ·
The decades fly,
The yearnings fade, the longings die.
You learn to bid them all good-bye.
And oh, the peace,
The blessed peace . . .
At last you come to know:

The roads you never take
Go through rocky ground,
Don't they?
The choices that you make
Aren't all that grim.
The worlds you never see
Still will be around,
Won't they?
The Ben I'll never be,
Who remembers him?

SALLY: I remember him. I even think I loved him once.

(Ben and Sally move off as lights come up on Buddy and Phyllis together on the gantry. Below them, on the stage, a few couples begin social dancing.)

BUDDY: Well, there they go, my Sally and your Ben. They make a lovely couple, don't they? You have any kids, Phyl?
PHYLLIS: None at all. Ben put it off, and then it was too late.
BUDDY: We've got two: Tom and Tim. Sally picked the names out. They're in San Francisco now and she gets lonely for them, so she calls them on the phone and fights. She's

fought with everyone she knows. Phyl, all I want is Sally back the way she used to be. I want the girl I married.

PHYLLIS: That's impossible, but never mind.

BUDDY: I begged her not to come tonight. It's happening again, the way I knew it would.

PHYLLIS: What is?

BUDDY: She's still in love with Ben.

PHYLLIS: I used to wonder but I never knew for sure. Times change. It might have mattered once.

(Young Ben and Young Phyllis emerge from the dancing couples. Phyllis sees them, Buddy doesn't. Phyllis, caught by surprise at the sweetness of her memory, watches.)

YOUNG PHYLLIS: Ben, I don't need a ring like this, it cost too much.

YOUNG BEN: It's nothing, Phyl; just half a carat. Give me time. The day will come I'll walk you into Tiffany's and buy the store.

YOUNG PHYLLIS: You'll never give me anything as beautiful as this.

YOUNG BEN: You'll make a good wife, Phyl.

YOUNG PHYLLIS: Good isn't good enough. I need to grow, I know that, and I will. I'll study and I'll read and walk my feet off in the Metropolitan Museum. You'll be so proud of me.

PHYLLIS: Oh my God . . .

BUDDY: What is it?

PHYLLIS: Bargains, Buddy. One makes bargains with one's life. That's what maturity amounts to. When we're young, there is no limit to the roles we hope to play—star, mother, hostess, hausfrau—all rolled into one. I learned to choose, to constantly select; as if each day were a painting and I had to get the colors right. We're careful of our colors, Ben and I, and what we've made is beautiful. I had a lover once. His name was Jack, I think. He played the drums and had long hair and no command of language. He was everything Ben wasn't, and we'd while away the afternoons with Gallo wine and one another, listening to the pop hits and the news. I thought it answered everything, but these things pass and I have sixty thousand dollars worth of Georgian silver in my dining room.

BUDDY: What happened to you Phyl?

PHYLLIS: I went my own damn way and don't make waves.

(Phyllis strides away from Buddy, who also leaves slowly in the opposite direction.

The social dancing evolves into the Danse d'Amore, during which the Young and Old Whitmans echo each other's steps.

As the dance finishes, focus moves to Sally and Ben.)

SALLY: . . . And Ben, I used to think a lot about the future; what I'd do or where I'd be or what if this or that dream never happened. All the things I thought made life worth living, they don't seem to matter much. I wanted a career once, but the Follies closed and nothing happened and you know what? I was fine. I wanted children and I had two gorgeous boys who did what boys do: they grew up and moved away. I miss them, but they're not the answer.

BEN: What is?

SALLY: Buddy. He's what makes life worth living.

(She sings:)

> Life is slow but it seems exciting
> 'Cause Buddy's there.
> Gourmet cooking and letter-writing
> And knowing Buddy's there.
> Every morning—don't faint—
> I tend the flowers. Can you believe it?
> Every weekend I paint

For umpteen hours.
And yes, I miss a lot
Living like a shut-in.
No, I haven't got
Cooks and cars and diamonds.
Yes, my clothes are not
Paris fashions, but in
Buddy's eyes,
I'm young, I'm beautiful.
In Buddy's eyes
I don't get older.
So life is ducky
And time goes flying
And I'm so lucky
I feel like crying,
And—

(Her voice catches as Young Ben and Young Sally appear.)

YOUNG SALLY *(Hurt and angry)*: No, Ben. Not now, not tonight,
not ever.

YOUNG BEN: You don't mean that, Sally.

YOUNG SALLY: You—you give a ring to her and mess around
with me. You can't play with people's feelings, not with
mine.

YOUNG BEN: I want you, you want me, you know it.

YOUNG SALLY *(Passionately)*: Oh, God, Ben . . .

(They go into each other's arms, then drift off.)

SALLY:

In Buddy's eyes,
I'm young, I'm beautiful.
In Buddy's eyes
I can't get older.
I'm still the princess,

Still the prize.
In Buddy's eyes,
I'm young, I'm beautiful.
In Buddy's arms,
On Buddy's shoulder,
I won't get older.
Nothing dies.
And all I ever dreamed I'd be,
The best I ever thought of me,
Is every minute there to see
In Buddy's eyes.

(The band strikes up a tune. Ben and Sally start to dance. Phyllis moves briskly to Ben and taps him on the shoulder.)

PHYLLIS: Ben, get me a refill, would you?

(Ben nods, moves off.)

Sally, wait. Don't go. *(Conversational)* Let's dish. Tell me everything. You ever miss New York? Where did you get your dress? What's the weather out in Phoenix? How do you like my husband?
SALLY: Ben? I've always liked him, you know that.
PHYLLIS: You find him changed?
SALLY: Not really, not down deep.
PHYLLIS: I rarely dip beneath the surface. Buddy thinks you're still in love with him.
SALLY: That man . . . he gets so jealous sometimes.
PHYLLIS: What of? That's the enigma of the week.
SALLY *(Squeezing Phyllis's arm)*: I'm sorry, I don't want to fight with you, Phyl. I don't have to.
PHYLLIS: Would you care to expand on that?

(There is a loud noise of girlish shrieks from offstage. Everyone enters, led by Weismann.)

STELLA *(Moving downstage with Sandra and Deedee)*: I'm not making an ass of myself alone. If I do the Mirror Number, we all do the Mirror Number. You, too, Phyllis.

SALLY: Oh, come on, Phyl. Join the fun. *(Does a tap step)* See? There's nothing to it, it's a snap.

PHYLLIS: If you can do it, I can do it.

DEEDEE: I wish my kids could see me now.

SANDRA: Would you believe it? I have stage fright.

CARLOTTA: I haven't danced in thirty years.

STELLA: Well, heaven help us.

(To the bandleader) Hit it, baby.

(She sings:)

> Who's that woman? I know her well,
> All decked out head to toe.
> She lives life like a carousel:
> Beau after beau after beau.
> Nightly, daily,
> Always laughing gaily,
> Seems I see her everywhere I go.
> Oh—
>
> Who's that woman?
> I know I know that woman,
> So clever, but ever so sad.
> Love, she said, was a fad.
> The kind of love that she couldn't make fun of
> She'd have none of.
>
> Who's that woman,
> That cheery, weary woman
> Who's dressing for yet one more spree?
> Each day I see her pass
> In my looking glass—
> Lord, lord, lord, that woman is me!

SALLY, PHYLLIS, STELLA, DEEDEE, SANDRA AND CARLOTTA:
> Mirror, mirror, on the wall,
> Who's the saddest gal in town?
> Who's been riding for a fall?
> Whose Lothario let her down?
> Mirror, mirror, answer me:
> Who is she who plays the clown?
> Is she out each night till three?
> Does she laugh with too much glee?
> On reflection, she'd agree.
> Mirror, mirror,
> Mirror, mirror,
> Mirror, mirror . . .

(The women are joined by their young selves. The sound of tap shoes, lots of them, in perfect precision, pick up the beat.)

STELLA:

SALLY, PHYLLIS, DEEDEE, SANDRA, CARLOTTA AND THEIR YOUNG SELVES:

Who's that woman?
I mean I've seen that woman
Who's joking but choking
Back tears.
All those glittering years
She thought that
Love was a matter of,
"Hi, there!"
"Kiss me!" "Bye, there!"
Who's that woman,
That cheery, weary woman,
Who's dressing for yet one
More spree?
The vision's getting blurred.
Isn't that absurd?

Mirror, mirror, on the wall,

Who's the saddest gal in town?

Who's been riding for a fall?

Love was a matter of,
"Hi, there!"
"Kiss me!" "Bye, there!"
Mirror, mirror, answer me.

Who is she who plays the clown?

Lord, lord, lord!	Lord, lord, lord!
Lord, lord, lord, lord, lord!	
That woman is me.	
	Mirror, mirror!
That woman is me.	
	Mirror, mirror!
That woman is me!	Mirror, mirror!
	Mirror!

(The guests break into loud applause. As it starts to die down:)

STELLA *(Winded)*: Wasn't that a blast? I love life, you know that. I've got my troubles and I take my lumps, we've got no kids, we never made much money and a lot of folks I love are dead, but on the whole and everything considered . . . Where was I? What the hell, I talk too much.

(Excited chatter rises as:)

SALLY *(Breathless, bubbling)*: Oh, Buddy, did you see me?
BUDDY: Kid, I couldn't take my eyes off you.
PHYLLIS: Well, Ben? Was I ravishing? You haven't said.
BEN: I'm speechless. How on earth did you remember?
PHYLLIS: I don't know. Unless it's muscle memory. It's curious, the things our bodies won't forget.
BEN: It sure is.

(Ben walks away from her. She follows as:)

BUDDY: It's been some party, hasn't it. How's Ben?
SALLY: I don't think Phyllis makes him happy. I see sadness in his eyes.
BUDDY: I'll bet you do.
SALLY: What's that supposed to mean?
BUDDY *(Swallowing his anger)*: Look, Sally, I've been thinking. I'm away too much. Why don't I tell them at the office that

I'm finished on the road. We could go out more, have some fun. I know I let you down sometimes, but I'll try harder. Honestly, I will. Come on, kid, let's go home.

SALLY: I wouldn't leave here for the world.

PHYLLIS: Ben?

BEN: Now's not a good time, Phyl.

PHYLLIS: That's right, turn off. My God, we haven't had an honest talk since '41. You think the Japs'll win the war?

BEN: I'm in no mood for honest talks.

PHYLLIS: I am. When did you love me last? Was it ten years ago or never? Do you ever contemplate divorce? Or suicide? Why don't you play around? Or do you? Have you cried much lately? Are you ever savaged by regret? Does one more day with me seem insupportable? Or are you dead?

BEN: I have my moments.

BUDDY: We've had a good life, kid.

SALLY: Since when?

BUDDY: Don't talk like that. What do you want from me? No matter what I do, it's never good enough. I come home feeling great and touch you and you look at me like I've been living in some sewer.

SALLY: Haven't you? You've always got a woman someplace. Oh, I know. You leave things in your pockets so I'll know.

BUDDY: She lives in Dallas and her name is—

SALLY: I don't want to hear it.

BUDDY: Margie! Margie—that's her name. She works at Neiman's and she's got a little house. It's quiet, we'll just sit and talk for hours. And she cooks for me and sews my buttons on and when we go to bed, it's like she thought I was some kind of miracle. She's twenty-nine and pretty and you know what my luck is? My luck is I love you. *(Strides angrily away)*

PHYLLIS: God, the way I wanted you when we were dating. Why did you want me? What was I? Just some chorus girl who lost it in a rumble seat? Don't you remember? You were there. Son of a bitch, I'm going to cry. *(No tears)*

BEN: You wore a gray dress and the zipper stuck, and all you did was sob about your mother and how she'd feel if she knew. You were terrific.

PHYLLIS: Listen, Ben. I've spent years wanting to be old. Imagine that. I couldn't wait till we were old enough so nothing mattered anymore. I've still got time for something in my life. I want another chance. I'm still young and I'm talking to the walls. Where are you?

BEN: Right where you are, and it's yes to all your questions. Yes, I loved you once and, yes, I play around and, yes, I have regrets and, God yes, one more day with you— *(He storms off)*

PHYLLIS *(Reaches for a drink from a passing waiter)*: I'll take that. You have a nice face. I don't suppose you play the drums.

(Phyllis follows the waiter off. Carlotta and Weismann are sitting engrossed in conversation.)

CARLOTTA: . . . So, Mitya, here's what it comes down to. Movies, Vegas, television: I'm a triple threat. I've done them all. But none of that compares to this. There's nothing like the shows we did here. Don't you miss it?

WEISMANN: Me? I always know when things are over. After this, I did some plays; then that was over. So I married once or twice and that was over. Now I've got an art collection, but sooner or later . . .

CARLOTTA: Tell me about it.

(She sings:)

> Good times and bum times,
> I've seen them all and, my dear,
> I'm still here.
> Plush velvet sometimes,
> Sometimes just pretzels and beer,
> But I'm here.

I've stuffed the dailies
In my shoes,
Strummed ukuleles,
Sung the blues,
Seen all my dreams disappear,
But I'm here.

I've slept in shanties, guest of the W.P.A.,
But I'm here.
Danced in my scanties,
Three bucks a night was the pay,
But I'm here.
I've stood on bread lines
With the best,
Watched while the headlines
Did the rest.
In the Depression was I depressed?
Nowhere near.
I met a big financier,
And I'm here.

I've been through Gandhi,
Windsor and Wally's affair,
And I'm here.
Amos 'n' Andy,
Mah-jongg and platinum hair,
And I'm here.
I got through *Abie's
Irish Rose,*
Five Dionne babies,
Major Bowes,
Had heebie-jeebies
For Beebe's
Bathysphere.
I lived through Shirley Temple
And I'm here.

I've gotten through Herbert and J. Edgar Hoover—
Gee, that was fun and a half.
When you've been through Herbert and J. Edgar
    Hoover,
Anything else is a laugh.

I've been through Reno,
I've been through Beverly Hills,
And I'm here.
Reefers and vino,
Rest cures, religion and pills,
But I'm here.
Been called a pinko
Commie tool,
Got through it stinko
By my pool.
I should have gone to an acting school,
That seems clear.
Still, someone said, "She's sincere,"
So I'm here.

Black sable one day,
Next day it goes into hock,
But I'm here.
Top billing Monday,
Tuesday you're touring in stock,
But I'm here.

First you're another
Sloe-eyed vamp,
Then someone's mother,
Then you're camp.
Then you career from career
To career.
I'm almost through my memoirs,
And I'm here.

I've gotten through, "Hey, lady, aren't you whoozis?
Wow! What a looker you were."
Or, better yet, "Sorry, I thought you were whoozis.
Whatever happened to her?"

Good times and bum times,
I've seen them all and, my dear,
I'm still here.
Plush velvet sometimes,
Sometimes just pretzels and beer,
But I'm here.
I've run the gamut
A to Z.
Three cheers and dammit,
C'est la vie.
I got through all of last year,
And I'm here.
Lord knows, at least I was there,
And I'm here!
Look who's here!
I'm still here!

(Lights rise on Ben and Sally talking and . . .)

BEN: Sally, truth to tell, the one impulsive thing I ever did was
marry Phyllis. We must have loved each other very much.
And these days? Why does she stay with me, for God's
sake? She despises me, you know.
SALLY: How do you bear it? Me, I read a lot—just trashy stuff,
to pass the time—and the amount of junk about love people write . . . When I loved you and you loved me . . . I
drift off sometimes. I just close my eyes and let it come.

(Ben closes his eyes.)

You feel anything?

BEN: Not much.

(Young Ben and Young Sally appear. He's bare to the waist, she wears a slip. They kiss each other passionately.)

YOUNG SALLY: I love you, Ben. I always will. You're the only one. I couldn't live without you, Ben. I'd kill myself.

BEN: I made love to a girl this afternoon. I do that now and then; it happens. After it was over, guess what? I began to cry. I would give—what have I got?—my soul's of little value, but I'd give it to be twenty-five again.

SALLY: It's not too late. It never is.

BEN: It's my life and I've lived it wrong.

SALLY: I know. I've always known.

SALLY AND YOUNG SALLY: Oh my sweet Ben.

YOUNG SALLY: I don't mind giving up the stage, and Buddy doesn't love me, not like you do. I can wait until the war is over.

BEN: Did I love you, Sally? Was it real?

SALLY AND YOUNG SALLY: I'll write you letters and I'll knit you socks. I'll go half crazy from the waiting but I'll stand it somehow. I can wait forever just so long as at the end of it there's you.

(Young Sally slips into Ben's arms. Sally moves into Young Ben's. Both couples mirror each other's movements. Ben sings to Young Sally:)

BEN:

> Too many mornings,
> Waking and pretending I reach for you.
> Thousands of mornings,
> Dreaming of my girl . . .
>
> All that time wasted,
> Merely passing through,

Time I could have spent,
So content
Wasting time with you.

Too many mornings,
Wishing that the room might be filled with you,
Morning to morning,
Turning into days.
All the days
That I thought would never end,
All the nights
With another day to spend,
All those times
I'd look up to see
Sally standing at the door,
Sally moving to the bed,
Sally resting in my arms
With her head against my head.

(Young Ben and Young Sally leave their partners and slip back into each other's arms.)

SALLY *(Speaks)*: If you don't kiss me, Ben, I think I'm going to die.

(Sally sings:)

How I planned:
What I'd wear tonight and
When should I get here,
How should I find you,
Where I'd stand,
What I'd say in case you
Didn't remember,
How I'd remind you—
You remembered,

And my fears were wrong!
Was it ever real?
Did I ever love you this much?
Did we ever feel
So happy then?

BEN: SALLY:
It was always real
                             I should have worn green.
And I've always loved you   I wore green the last time,
    this much.
We can always feel
                             The time I
This happy . . .   Was happy . . .

SALLY AND BEN:
Too many mornings
Wasted in pretending I reach for you,
How many mornings
Are there still to come?

How much time can we hope that there will be?
Not much time, but it's time enough for me,
If there's time to look up and see
Sally standing at the door,
Sally moving to the bed,
Sally resting in your/my arms,
With your head against my head.

(Sally falls into Ben's arms. The couples are in identical
embraces. They kiss.
    Curtain.)

ACT II

The entr'acte music ends.

The curtain rises. Sally, Ben, Young Sally and Young Ben are exactly as we left them, but now Buddy and Young Buddy are observing them from a distance. The final bars of music fade away, the embrace ends.

BEN: I want you, Sally.

SALLY: Ben, I know you do.

BEN: I want you now. This minute. Come on, let's get out of here.

SALLY: Just one thing, Ben. We're getting married, aren't we? I mean, this time you're going to marry me.

YOUNG SALLY: You love me, Ben. Let's get married now. She can't love you like I do.

BEN: Oh my God, what am I doing?

YOUNG BEN: Just give me time.

YOUNG SALLY: There isn't any time. You're shipping out.

SALLY: We'll be so happy.

YOUNG SALLY: What if you don't come back?

YOUNG BEN: Lawyers don't get shot.

YOUNG SALLY: Ben, marry me.

BEN AND YOUNG BEN: Sally, listen.

SALLY: I'll make you the best wife.

YOUNG SALLY: Now, if you really love me.

YOUNG BEN: Love you, yes, I love you.

YOUNG SALLY: Then why not?

BEN: Sally, listen to me. Stop . . .

YOUNG BEN: I have to leave.

BEN: Please, we have to talk . . .

SALLY *(Kissing Ben)*: Silly Ben. It's all right.

YOUNG SALLY: I want a reason.

YOUNG BEN: Quit pressing me.

SALLY: I'll get my wrap and we can leave.

YOUNG SALLY: Look at me, dammit!

(Young Ben exits.)

BEN: Sally, wait.

SALLY: I'm so happy.

(Sally exits.)

YOUNG SALLY: You turn around and look at me.

(Ben and Young Sally exit in opposite directions. Young Buddy moves downstage.)

YOUNG BUDDY: No!

(Buddy moves downstage, mirroring his young self.)

BUDDY: What the hell do I see in her for Chrissake? I knew all that was going on. *(Turns on his young self)* Why the hell did I marry her?

(Young Buddy walks away slowly. Buddy sings:)

The right girl—yeah!
The right girl,
She makes you feel like a million bucks
Instead of—what?—like a rented tux.

The right girl—yeah!
The right girl,
She's with you, no matter how you feel,
You're not the good guy, you're not the heel.
You're not the dreamboat that sank—you're real
When you got—
The right girl—yeah!
And I got—

(He has no words for what he's got. Instead, he bursts into an angry dance, leaping down stairs, twisting, tapping without tap shoes all the fury and regret he feels. Then, without preparation, the music changes and the anger's gone and he sings:)

Hey, Margie, I'm back, babe.
Come help me unpack, babe.
Hey, Margie, hey, bright girl,
I'm home.

What's new, babe? You miss me?
You smell good, come kiss me.
Hey, Margie, you wanna go dancing?
I'm home.

Des Moines was rotten and the deal fell through.
I pushed, babe.
I'm bushed, babe.
I needed you to tell my troubles to—
The heck, babe—
Let's neck, babe.

Hey, Margie,
You wanna go dancing?
You wanna go driving? Or something?
Okay, babe,
Whatever you say, babe—
You wanna stay home!
You wanna stay home!

*(He holds an imagined Margie in his arms and dances with
her tenderly; then:)*

Hey, Margie, it's day, babe,
My flight goes—no, stay, babe,
You know how you cry, babe—
Stay home.

Be good, now, we'll speak, babe,
It might be next week, babe—
Hey, Margie—good-bye, babe—
I gotta go home.

(The angry music of the opening returns.)

The right girl—yeah!
The right girl,
She sees you're nothing and thinks you're king,
She knows you got other songs to sing.
You still could be—hell, well, anything
When you got—yeah!
The right girl—
And I got . . .

(The music becomes tender again.)

Hey, Margie, I'm back, babe.
Come help me unpack, babe.

Hey, Margie, hey, bright girl,
I'm home.
You miss me? I knew it.
Hey, Margie, I blew it—
I don't love the right girl.

Ah, shit . . .

(Final chord. Sally enters.)

SALLY: Buddy.

BUDDY: Sally . . . The mess, the moods, the spells you get, in bed for days without a word. Or else you're crying, God, the tears around our place—or flying out to Tom or Tim and camping at their doorstep just to fight. It's crazy and—we're finished, kid; that's all she wrote. It's over.

SALLY: Don't feel bad, darling. You'll be better off without me and I'm going to be just fine. You see, Ben wants to marry me. He asked me if I'd marry him and naturally I said I would.

BUDDY: Marry you? You're either drunk or crazy and I don't care which.

SALLY: He took me in his arms and kissed me. I know every word he said.

BUDDY *(In a rage)*: I've spent my whole life making things the way you want them and no matter what we do or where we go or what we've got, it isn't what you want. It used to drive me nuts. Not anymore. So you wake up hung over or you wake up in the funny farm, it's all the goddamn same to me.

(Buddy storms off.)

SALLY: He held me and the band was playing. I'm getting married and I'm going to live forever with the man I love. Oh, dear Lord, isn't it a wonder?

(Lights fade. They come up on Ben and Carlotta. She is laughing, soft and throaty. He sits near her, tense, desperate and fairly drunk.)

BEN: Just meet me later. I don't want to be alone, that's all.

CARLOTTA: You're married; you can play around. I'm in between; I never cheat on guys I'm living with.

BEN: I only want to talk.

CARLOTTA: Come on, come on now; you're a big boy.

BEN: Right you are. I'll tell you fascinating tales of my adventures, make you laugh.

CARLOTTA: It's nothing; you'll feel better in the morning.

BEN: Take me home and hold me—Jesus, please.

CARLOTTA: We had some fun once; it was just a thing. That's all you meant to me, Ben, just a thing. *(She gently touches his hair)* The guy I'm living with, he's just a thing, too. But he's twenty-six. I like him. I liked you. Next year I'll like some other guy. Men are so sweet.

(Focus shifts to another area of the stage where a couple is necking. Soon we see that the couple is Phyllis and Kevin, the waiter she spoke with earlier. He is kissing her neck.)

PHYLLIS *(Looking at nothing)*: I used to wish I had a son. I was going to call him Eddie, and I used to go to shops to look for things for him to wear. I'd see a nightshirt on the counter, pick it up and hold it in my hands—young man, you're getting me all wet.

KEVIN: Now, that's a hell of a remark.

PHYLLIS: I don't know what we're doing here.

KEVIN *(Feelings hurt)*: This wasn't my idea. You started it.

PHYLLIS: All right, all right; you've been assaulted by a crazy lady. Where's a drink?

KEVIN: I'll get you one.

PHYLLIS: Come here. *(He hesitates)* The moon's gone down; you're safe. *(As he brings her a drink)* Now that we've been introduced; tell me: do you find me attractive?

KEVIN: I dunno—Yeah, I do. It beats me.

PHYLLIS: Thanks. Do you sleep around a lot?

KEVIN: Sure, all the time.

PHYLLIS: Do you find, in your experience, does that make sex less pleasurable?

KEVIN: Does what?

PHYLLIS: Not loving anyone.

KEVIN: Hell, I dunno. I never think about it.

PHYLLIS *(Her face starts to fall apart)*: That's a neat trick.

KEVIN: Hey, lady, what's the matter?

PHYLLIS: If I knew, I'd have it fixed.

(Phyllis turns away from Kevin, who leaves her as the lights fade.

Elsewhere, a spotlight picks up Heidi, who sits lost in reverie. She sings "One More Kiss." Midway, Young Heidi appears, and the song becomes a duet, an old voice and a young one, entwined.)

HEIDI:

>One more kiss before we part,
>One more kiss and—farewell,
>Never shall we meet again,
>Just a kiss and then
>We break the spell.

>One more kiss to melt the heart,
>One more glimpse of the past,

HEIDI AND YOUNG HEIDI:

>One more souvenir of bliss,
>Knowing well that this
>One must be the last.

Dreams are a sweet mistake.
All dreamers must awake.

YOUNG HEIDI:

On, then, with the dance,
No backward glance
Or my heart will break.
Never look back.

HEIDI:	YOUNG HEIDI:
Never look back.	
One more kiss before we part.	Ah . . . ah . . .
	Not with tears or a sigh.
All things beautiful must die	All things beautiful must die
	Now that our love is done,
Lover, give me . . .	

HEIDI AND YOUNG HEIDI:

. . . One
More kiss and—good-bye.

*(Lights fade on Heidi and Young Heidi as they walk away.
Lights come up on Phyllis as she approaches Ben.)*

PHYLLIS: Well, don't you look moody.

BEN: I've been thinking.

PHYLLIS: That makes two of us. Ben, do you know, according
to statistics, I can't expect to die for thirty years. That's
one long time and I've been analyzing what my options
are. Hell, even on the gallows, there are choices: you can
take it like a man or cry a lot. What's there for me? It all
comes down to this: I won't go back to what we've had,
not one more day of it.

BEN: How right you are. I don't know how I've stood it all these
years. The only thing I want from you is a divorce.

PHYLLIS: Get him: puppy love at fifty-three. I see you both in your bikinis, honeymooning at Boca Raton. She'll be a hit at the foundation in her tap shoes.

BEN: Hell, I've never been in love with Sally, not in any way that matters. There's no one in my life; there's nothing. That's what's killing me.

PHYLLIS: I'm nothing. That's not much.

BEN: God, I see lovers on the street—it's real, it's going on out there and I can't reach it. Someone's got to love me and I don't care if it doesn't last a month, I don't care if I'm ludicrous or who she is or what she's like.

PHYLLIS: You haven't got a clue what love is. I should have left you years ago.

BEN: Leave me now. That's all I want. Just pack a bag and disappear.

(Phyllis sings:)

PHYLLIS:

    Leave you? Leave you?
    How could I leave you?
    How could I go it alone?
    Could I wave the years away
    With a quick good-bye?
    How do you wipe tears away
    When your eyes are dry?

    Sweetheart, lover,
    Could I recover,
    Give up the joys I have known?
    Not to fetch your pills again
    Every day at five,
    Not to give those dinners for ten
    Elderly men
    From the U.N.—
    How could I survive?

Could I leave you
And your shelves of the world's best books
And the evenings of martyred looks,
Cryptic sighs,
Sullen glares from those injured eyes?
Leave the quips with a sting, jokes with a sneer,
Passionless lovemaking once a year?
Leave the lies ill concealed
And the wounds never healed
And the games not worth winning
And—wait, I'm just beginning!

What, leave you, leave you,
How could I leave you?
What would I do on my own?
Putting thoughts of you aside
In the south of France,
Would I think of suicide?
Darling, shall we dance?

Could I live through the pain
On a terrace in Spain?
Would it pass? It would pass.
Could I bury my rage
With a boy half your age
In the grass? Bet your ass.
But I've done that already—or didn't you know, love?
Tell me, how could I leave when I left long ago, love?

Could I leave you?
No, the point is, could you leave me?
Well, I guess you could leave me the house,
Leave me the flat,
Leave me the Braques and Chagalls and all that.
You could leave me the stocks for sentiment's sake
And ninety percent of the money you make,

And the rugs
And the cooks—
Darling, you keep the drugs,
Angel, you keep the books,
Honey, I'll take the grand,
Sugar, you keep the spinet
And all of our friends and
Just wait a goddamn minute!

Oh, leave you? Leave you?
How could I leave you?
Sweetheart, I have to confess:
Could I leave you?
Yes.
Will I leave you?
Will *I* leave *you*?
Guess!

BEN: My hands, they won't stop shaking.

(Young Ben and Young Phyllis appear.)

YOUNG BEN: You'll make a good wife, Phyl.
YOUNG PHYLLIS: I'll try. Oh, Ben, I'll try so hard. I'm not
    much now, I know that, but I'll study and I'll read and I'll
    walk my feet off in the Metropolitan Museum.
PHYLLIS: I tried so hard. I studied and I read. I thought I wasn't
    much—I was terrific. And I walked my goddamn feet off.
    (Turning to Young Phyllis) What happened to you, Phyl?
YOUNG PHYLLIS: I love you, Ben.
BEN *(To Young Ben)*: She did—and what did you give her?
YOUNG BEN: Someday I'll have the biggest goddamn limousine.
BEN *(To Young Ben with loathing)*: You were so smart.
PHYLLIS *(To Young Phyllis)*: Where did you go?
YOUNG PHYLLIS: We've got each other, Ben. What difference
    does it make?

BEN *(To Young Ben)*: You had it all and you threw it away.

(Buddy enters, steaming.)

BUDDY: You bastard.
BEN *(Wrenching himself into the present)*: What?
BUDDY: You fourteen-carat bastard.

(Young Buddy enters.)

YOUNG BUDDY: You're my best friend, best I ever had, Ben.
BEN *(To Buddy)*: What's all this about?
BUDDY: You know damn well what this is about.
YOUNG BUDDY: You wouldn't screw around with Sally. Take
    her dancing maybe but that's all, right?
BEN: I don't understand.
BUDDY: Yes, you do.
YOUNG BUDDY: That's all—right, Ben?
YOUNG BEN: She's a sweet kid but that's where it stops.
BUDDY: What did you do to her?
YOUNG BUDDY: You're a goddamn liar.
YOUNG BEN: Screw you.
SALLY *(Appearing with Young Sally; to Ben)*: It's getting late,
    Ben. We should go.
PHYLLIS *(To Ben)*: You're not in love with Sally. Boy, you take
    the cake.
SALLY: Have you told Phyl yet?
BEN: But I never said I loved you, did I?
YOUNG SALLY: Now, if you really love me.
YOUNG BEN: Love you, yes I love you.
YOUNG SALLY: Then why not?
BEN: I'm sorry. I never meant to hurt you, but, Sally, it was fin-
    ished years ago.
YOUNG BUDDY *(To Young Sally)*: You really love me, don't
    you, kid?
YOUNG SALLY: With all my heart, Buddy . . .

BUDDY *(To Young Sally)*: That's a lie.

SALLY: Please, Ben, I'd like to go now.

BUDDY *(To Sally)*: Ben ran out and I was there. That's all it was.

YOUNG SALLY *(To Young Ben)*: I want a reason. Am I cheap? Is that it? I'm not good enough.

YOUNG BEN: Think what you goddamn please.

YOUNG SALLY: Don't leave me, Ben.

SALLY *(Turning on Young Sally)*: You fool!

YOUNG PHYLLIS: I want a baby, Ben.

SALLY *(To Young Sally)*: You could have had him, but you played it wrong.

YOUNG PHYLLIS *(To Young Ben)*: Ben, can't we have one, can't we try?

(Sally and Buddy speak simultaneously.)

SALLY *(To Young Sally)*: You had him crazy for you but you let him up your skirts too soon!

BUDDY *(To Young Buddy)*: You took her back. She two-timed you and you married her.

(Phyllis and Ben speak simultaneously.)

PHYLLIS *(To Ben)*: I now see right through you. Hollow, that's what you are. You're an empty place.

BEN *(To Young Ben)*: You never loved her. Why'd you marry her? Because it made sense? Is that all for chrissake?

(All four speak simultaneously, each of them turning on their past self with mounting rage as if they mean to do physical violence to the memories.)

Smart. You knew what you were doing: both eyes open. You can't spend your life with someone you don't love. It's crazy. You unfeeling bastard on the make. Look what you've done to me!

BUDDY *(To Young Buddy)*: She never loved you and you knew it. In your guts you damn well knew it. What did you expect for chrissakes? Married to a girl like that. You pissed my life away that's what you did to me.

PHYLLIS *(To Young Phyllis)*: He never loved you and you knew it. Deep down you knew. You thought he'd change if you loved him enough. You silly bitch, you fool. You threw my life away!

SALLY *(To Young Sally)*: The only man I ever wanted, and you lost him for me. Everything, you lost me everything. You tramp. You left me here with nothing. I could kill you. I could die!

(All eight at once. It's now senseless, and frightening.)

YOUNG BUDDY *(To Young Sally)*: Baby I love you so much. The moon, I'll buy it for you. Everything you ever wanted, baby, that's what Buddy's going to get for you.

YOUNG SALLY *(To Young Buddy)*: Honey, you're the only one. The things you do to me. The way you make me feel. I love it, Buddy. Geez, I love you.

YOUNG PHYLLIS *(To Young Ben)*: Dearest, oh my dearest Ben, I'll be so good for you, you'll be so happy. I'll be everything you ever wanted, just for you.

YOUNG BEN *(To Young Phyllis)*: Darling, to the top. That's where we're going: straight up and the view from there, the view is something.

BUDDY *(To Young Buddy)*: I could have had a great life all along. I had the wrong wife, that was all. You've screwed me and I'll get you for it!

SALLY *(To Young Sally)*: I'll pay you back, that's what I'll do. For all the things I never had. You're gonna pay!

PHYLLIS *(To Young Phyllis)*: I've had no life—I haven't lived. You can't do what you've done to me and get away with it!

BEN *(To Young Ben)*: You killed me—I've been dead for thirty years. It's all your work—you did it!

(As the madness of the confrontation hits its peak, heavenly music is heard and we find ourselves transported to Loveland: a Ziegfeld extravaganza, complete with costumed Chorus and a bevy of Showgirls. The Chorus sings as the eight protagonists are swallowed up in the celebration:)

CHORUS:
> Time stops, hearts are young,
> Only serenades are sung
> In Loveland,
> Where everybody lives to love.

> Raindrops never rain,
> Every road is Lover's Lane
> In Loveland,
> Where everybody loves to live.

> See that sunny sun and honeymoon,
> There where seven hundred days hath June.

> Sweetheart, take my hand,
> Let us find that wondrous land
> Called Loveland, Loveland, Loveland . . .

FIRST SHOWGIRL:
> L is for the Long Long road ahead
> That leads all lovers to the landscape of their dreams.

CHORUS:
> Loveland,
> Where everybody lives to love.

SECOND SHOWGIRL:
> O is for the Overwhelming Optimism
> Only lovers know, or so it seems.

CHORUS:

> Loveland,
> Where everybody loves to live.

THIRD SHOWGIRL:

> V is for the Various Vicissitudes they'll weather,
> Because it's also for the vow they made together.

CHORUS:

> Loveland, Loveland . . .

FOURTH SHOWGIRL:

> E is for the Endless Expectations
> Lovers elevate so often to extremes.

CHORUS:

> Loveland, Loveland . . .

FIFTH SHOWGIRL:

> L is for the Lies that get perfected,
> A is for the Aims that go awry.

CHORUS:

> Loveland,
> Where everybody lives to love.

SIXTH SHOWGIRL:

> N is for the Needs that get neglected,
> D is for the Doubts that never die.

CHORUS:

> Loveland,
> Where everybody loves to live.
>
> Lovers pine and sigh but never part.
> Time is measured by a beating heart.

Bells ring, fountains splash,
Folks use kisses 'stead of cash
In Loveland, Loveland . . .

Love, Love, Loveland . . .
Love, Love, Loveland . . .
Love!

(The Young Lovers sing:)

YOUNG BEN:
"What will tomorrow bring?"
The pundits query.

YOUNG PHYLLIS:
Will it be cheery?

YOUNG BEN:
Will it be sad?

YOUNG PHYLLIS:
Will it be birds in spring
Or hara-kiri?

YOUNG BEN:
Don't worry, dearie.

YOUNG PHYLLIS:
Don't worry, lad.

YOUNG BEN:
I'll have our future
Suit your
Whim,
Blue chip preferred.

YOUNG PHYLLIS:
Putting it in a
Syno-

Nym,
Perfect's the word.

YOUNG BEN AND YOUNG PHYLLIS:
We're in this thing together,
Aren'tcha glad?
Each day from now will be
The best day you ever had.

YOUNG BEN:
You're gonna love tomorrow.

YOUNG PHYLLIS:
Mm-hm.

YOUNG BEN:
You're gonna be with me.

YOUNG PHYLLIS:
Mm-hm.

YOUNG BEN:
You're gonna love tomorrow,
I'm giving you my personal guarantee.

YOUNG PHYLLIS:
Say toodle-oo to sorrow.

YOUNG BEN:
Mm-hm.

YOUNG PHYLLIS:
And fare-thee-well, ennui.

YOUNG BEN:
Bye-bye.

YOUNG PHYLLIS:

    You're gonna love tomorrow,
    As long as your tomorrow is spent with me.

YOUNG BEN AND YOUNG PHYLLIS:

    Today was perfectly perfect,
    You say.
    Well, don't go away,
    'Cause if you think you liked today,

    You're gonna *love* tomorrow.
    Mm-hm.
    You stick around and see.

YOUNG PHYLLIS:

    Mm-hm.

YOUNG BEN AND YOUNG PHYLLIS:

    And if you love tomorrow,
    Then think of how it's gonna be:
    Tomorrow's what you're gonna have a lifetime of
    With me!

(Young Phyllis and Young Ben dance gaily off as Young Buddy and Young Sally dance on, hand in hand, and sing:)

YOUNG BUDDY:

    Sally, dear,
    Now that we're
    Man and wife,
    I will do
    Wonders to
    Make your life
    Soul-stirring
    And free of care.

YOUNG SALLY:
>If we fight
>(And we might),
>I'll concede.
>Furthermore,
>Dear, should your
>Ego need
>Bolstering,
>I'll do my share.

YOUNG BUDDY:
>But though I'll do my utmost
>To see you never frown,

YOUNG SALLY:
>And though I'll try to cut most
>Of our expenses down,

YOUNG BUDDY:
>I've some traits, I warn you,
>To which you'll have objections.

YOUNG SALLY:
>I, too, have a cornu-
>Copia of imperfections.

>I may burn the toast.

YOUNG BUDDY:
>Oh, well,
>I may make a rotten host.

YOUNG SALLY:
>Do tell.

YOUNG BUDDY AND YOUNG SALLY:
>But no matter what goes wrong,
>Love will see us through
>Till something better comes along.

YOUNG BUDDY:
>I may vex your folks.

YOUNG SALLY:
>Okay.
>I may interrupt your jokes.

YOUNG BUDDY:
>You may.

YOUNG BUDDY AND YOUNG SALLY:
>But if I come on too strong,
>Love will see us through
>Till something better comes along.

YOUNG BUDDY:
>I may play cards all night
>And come home at three.

YOUNG SALLY:
>Just leave a light
>On the porch for me.

YOUNG BUDDY AND YOUNG SALLY:
>Well, nobody's perfect!

YOUNG SALLY:
>I may trump your ace.

YOUNG BUDDY:
>Please do.
>I may clutter up the place.

YOUNG SALLY:
>Me, too.

YOUNG BUDDY AND YOUNG SALLY:
> But the minute we embrace
> To love's old sweet song,
> Dear, that will see us through
> Till something better comes along.

(Young Ben and Young Phyllis reenter.)

YOUNG SALLY:
> Hi.

YOUNG BEN:
> Girls.

YOUNG PHYLLIS:
> Ben.

YOUNG BUDDY:
> Sally.

YOUNG BEN:
> You're gonna love tomorrow

YOUNG SALLY:
> I may burn the toast.

YOUNG PHYLLIS:
> Mm-hm,

YOUNG BUDDY:
> Oh, well,
> I may make a rotten host.

YOUNG BEN:
> You're gonna be with me.

YOUNG SALLY:
> Do tell.

YOUNG PHYLLIS:
> Mm-hm.

YOUNG BEN:
> You're gonna love tomorrow
> I'm giving you my personal
> Guarantee.

YOUNG BUDDY AND
YOUNG SALLY:
> But no matter what goes wrong,
> Love will see us through
> Till something better comes
> Along.

YOUNG PHYLLIS:
Say toodle-oo to sorrow.

YOUNG BUDDY:
I may vex your folks.

YOUNG BEN:
Mm-hm.

YOUNG SALLY:
Okay.
I may interrupt your jokes.

YOUNG PHYLLIS:
And fare-thee-well, ennui.

YOUNG BUDDY:

You may.

YOUNG BEN:
Bye-bye.

YOUNG PHYLLIS:

You're gonna love tomorrow,
As long as your tomorrow is
Spent with me.

YOUNG BUDDY AND
   YOUNG SALLY:
But if I come on too strong,
Love will see us through
Till something better comes
Along.

YOUNG BEN AND
   YOUNG PHYLLIS:
Today was perfectly perfect,
You say.

YOUNG BUDDY:

I may play cards all night
And come home at three.

YOUNG SALLY:
Just leave a light
On the porch for me!

Well, don't go away,
'Cause if you think you liked
Today,

YOUNG BUDDY AND
   YOUNG SALLY:
Well, nobody's perfect!

| | YOUNG SALLY: |
| You're gonna love tomorrow. | I may trump your ace. |

	YOUNG BUDDY:
Mm-hm.	Please do.
	I may clutter up the place.
You stick around and see.	

| | YOUNG SALLY: |
| Mm-hm. | Me, too. |

	YOUNG BUDDY AND
	YOUNG SALLY:
And if you love tomorrow,	But the minute we embrace
Then think of how it's	To love's old sweet song,
Gonna be.	
Tomorrow's what you're	Dear, that will see us through
Gonna have,	Till something,
And Monday's what you're	Love will help us hew
Gonna have,	To something,
And love is what you're	Love will have to do
Gonna have	Till something
A lifetime of	Better comes
With me!	Along!

(A show curtain drops in downstage as the number ends. Buddy pops his head through the curtain, grins at us engagingly and sings:)

BUDDY:

      Hello, folks, we're into the Follies!
      First, though, folks, we'll pause for a mo'.
      No, no, folks, you'll still get your jollies—
      It's just I got a problem that I think you should know.
      See, I've been very perturbed of late, very upset,
      Very betwixt and between.

The things that I want, I don't seem to get.
The things that I get—you know what I mean?

(He steps through the curtain into full view. He is in his Follies costume now: plaid baggy pants, garish jacket and a shiny derby hat.)

I've got those
"God-why-don't-you-love-me-oh-you-do-I'll-see-you-
    later"
Blues,
That
"Long-as-you-ignore-me-you're-the-only-thing-that-
    matters"
Feeling,
That
"If-I'm-good-enough-for-you-you're-not-good-enough-
    and-thank-you-for-the-present-but-what's-wrong-`
    with-it?" stuff,
Those
"Don't-come-any-closer-'cause-you-know-how-much-
    I-love-you"
Feelings,
Those
"Tell-me-that-you-love-me-oh-you-did-I-gotta-run-
    now"
Blues.

(A Chorus Girl comes flouncing on, as a caricature of his beloved Margie.)

Margie! Oh, Margie!
She says she really loves me.

"MARGIE":
    I love you,

71

BUDDY:
>   —She says.
>   She says she really cares.

"MARGIE":
>   I care. I care.

BUDDY:
>   She says that I'm her hero.

"MARGIE":
>   My hero.

BUDDY:
>   —She says.
>   I'm perfect, she swears.

"MARGIE":
>   You're perfect, goddammit.

BUDDY:
>   She says that if we parted,

"MARGIE":
>   If we parted—?

BUDDY:
>   —She says,
>   She says that she'd be sick.

"MARGIE":
>   Bleah.

BUDDY:
>   She says she's mine forever—

"MARGIE":
>   Forever.

BUDDY:
    —She says.
    I gotta get outta here quick!

    I've got those
    "Whisper-how-I'm-better-than-I-think-but-what-do-
        you-know?"
    Blues,
    That
    "Why-do-you-keep-telling-me-I-stink-when-I-adore-
        you"
    Feeling,
    That
    "Say-I'm-all-the-world-to-you-you're-out-of-your-mind-
        I-know-there's-someone-else-and-I-could-kiss-your-
        behind,"
    Those
    "You-say-I'm-terrific-but-your-taste-was-always-
        rotten"
    Feelings,
    Those
    "Go-away-I-need-you,"
    "Come-to-me-I'll-kill-you,"
    "Darling-I'll-do-anything-to-keep-you-with-me-till-you-
        tell-me-that-you-love-me-oh-you-did-now-beat-it-
        will-you?"
    Blues!

(Another Chorus Girl, this time a cartoon of Sally, hip-swings her way onstage.)

    Sally! Oh, Sally!
    She says she loves another—

"SALLY":
    Another—

BUDDY:
>—She says,
>A fella she prefers.

"SALLY":
>Furs. Furs.

BUDDY:
>She says that he's her idol.

"SALLY":
>Idolidolidolidol—

BUDDY:
>—She says.
>Ideal, she avers.

"SALLY":
>You deal . . . "avers"?

BUDDY:
>She says that anybody—

"SALLY":
>Buddy—Bleah!—

BUDDY:
>—She says,
>Would suit her more than I.

"SALLY":
>Aye, aye, aye.

BUDDY:
>She says that I'm a washout—

"SALLY" *(Mouthed):*
     A washout—

BUDDY:
     —She says,
     I love her so much, I could die!
"SALLY"*(Spoken):* Get outta here!

     *(Buddy tears around the stage trying to catch her. "Margie"
     returns from the wings.)*

     Ooh. Ooh.
     Go 'way! Go 'way!
     Ah! Ah!

     *(There is a collision involving all three of them and, when
     they untangle themselves, they sing:)*

BUDDY:
     I've got those

BUDDY, "MARGIE" AND "SALLY":
     "God-why-don't-you-love-me-oh-you-do-I'll-see-you-
          later"
     Blues—

"MARGIE" AND "SALLY":
     Bla-bla-blues—!

BUDDY, "MARGIE" AND "SALLY":
     That
     "Long-as-you-ignore-me-you're-the-only-thing-that-
          matters"
     Feeling—

75

"MARGIE" AND "SALLY":
     Feeling—!

BUDDY:
     That
     "If-I'm-good-enough-for-you-you're-not-good-
          enough"—

"MARGIE" AND "SALLY":
     Woo—!

BUDDY:
     And "Thank-you-for-the-present-but-what's-wrong-
          with-it?" stuff,

"MARGIE" AND "SALLY":
     Oh—!

BUDDY:
     Those
     "Don't-come-any-closer-'cause-you-know-how-much-
          I-love-you"
     Feelings,

"MARGIE" AND "SALLY":
     Bla-bla-blues—!

BUDDY:	"MARGIE" AND "SALLY":
Those	
"If-you-will-then-I-can't,	
If-you-don't-then-I-gotta,	
Give-it-to-me-I-don't-want-it,	
If-you-won't-I-gotta-have-it,	
High-low-wrong-right-	
Yes-no-black-white,	
God-why-don't-you-love-me-	"Fast-slow-kiss-fight-
oh-you-do-I'll-see-you-later"	Stay-go-up-tight"

BUDDY, "MARGIE" AND "SALLY":
Blues!

(The number ends as they chase one another offstage. The lights dim down, the show curtain parts just enough to form a graceful frame, and standing there is Sally. She is costumed in a clinging, beaded silver gown, as if she were a screen seductress from the 1930s. Standing very still, she sings:)

SALLY:
The sun comes up,
I think about you.
The coffee cup,
I think about you.
I want you so,
It's like I'm losing my mind.

The morning ends,
I think about you.
I talk to friends,
I think about you.
And do they know?
It's like losing my mind.

All afternoon,
Doing every little chore,
The thought of you stays bright.
Sometimes I stand
In the middle of the floor,
Not going left,
Not going right.

I dim the lights
And think about you,
Spend sleepless nights

To think about you.
You said you loved me,
Or were you just being kind?
Or am I losing my mind?

I want you so,
It's like losing my mind.
Does no one know?
It's like losing my mind.

All afternoon,
Doing every little chore,
The thought of you stays bright.
Sometimes I stand
In the middle of the floor,
Not going left,
Not going right.

I dim the lights
And think about you,
Spend sleepless nights
To think about you.
You said you loved me,
Or were you just being kind?
Or am I losing my mind?

(The lights dim. We can just see Sally's face in the pinpoint spotlight as the curtain gently closes. There is a jazzy blare of trumpets, the lights abruptly rise, and Phyllis struts onstage wearing a short, fringe-skirted, bright red dress that exposes long and shapely legs. She throws a knowing grin at us and sings, as a gaggle of Chorus Boys enter to back her up:)

PHYLLIS:

Here's a little story that should make you cry,
About two unhappy dames.

Let us call them Lucy "X" and Jessie "Y,"
Which are not their real names.
Now Lucy has the purity
Along with the unsurety
That comes with being only twenty-one.
Jessie has maturity
And plenty of security.
Whatever you can do with them she's done.
Given their advantages,
You may ask why
The two ladies have such grief.
This is my belief,
In brief:

Lucy is juicy
But terribly drab.
Jessie is dressy
But cold as a slab.
Lucy wants to be dressy,
Jessie wants to be juicy
Lucy wants to be Jessie,
And Jessie Lucy.
You see,
Jessie is racy
But hard as a rock.
Lucy is lacy
But dull as a smock.
Jessie wants to be lacy,
Lucy wants to be Jessie.
That's the sorrowful précis.
It's very messy.

Poor sad souls,
Itching to be switching roles.
Lucy wants to do what Jessie does,
Jessie wants to be what Lucy was.

Lucy's a lassie
You pat on the head.
Jessie is classy
But virtually dead.
Lucy wants to be classy,
Jessie wants to be Lassie.
If Lucy and Jessie could only combine,
I could tell you someone
Who would finally feel just fine!

CHORUS BOYS:

Now if you see Lucy "X,"
Youthful, truthful Lucy "X,"
Let her know she's better than she suspects.
Now if you see Jessie "Y,"
Faded, jaded Jessie "Y,"
Tell her that she's sweller than apple pie.
Juicy Lucy,
Dressy Jessie,
Tell them that they ought to get together quick,
'Cause getting it together is the whole trick!

(She exits with the Chorus Boys and is replaced with a line of Chorus Girls as a curtain drops behind them. They sing:)

CHORUS:

Here he comes,
Mister Whiz.
Sound the drums,
Here he is.

Raconteur,
Bon vivant.
Tell us, sir,
What we want
To know:

The modus operandi
A dandy
Should use
When he is feeling low.

(The curtain rises, revealing Ben in a smoking jacket, looking pleased with himself and surrounded by other Chorus Girls and Boys. He sings:)

BEN:

When the winds are blowing,

CHORUS:

Yes?

BEN:

That's the time to smile.

CHORUS:

Oh?

BEN:

Learn how to laugh,
Learn how to love, learn how to live,
That's my style.
When the rent is owing . . .

CHORUS:

Yes?

BEN:

What's the use of tears?

CHORUS:

Oh?

BEN:

I'd rather laugh,
I'd rather love,
I'd rather live
In arrears.

Some fellows sweat
To get to be millionaires,
Some have a sport
They're devotees of.
Some like to be the champs
At saving postage stamps,
Me, I like to live,
Me, I like to laugh,
Me, I like to love.

Some like to sink
And think in their easy chairs
Of all the things
They've risen above.
Some like to be profound
By reading Proust and Pound.
Me, I like to live,
Me, I like to laugh,
Me, I like to love.

Success is swell
And success is sweet,
But every height has a drop.
The less achievement,
The less defeat.
What's the point of shovin'
Your way to the top?
Live 'n' laugh 'n' love 'n'
You're never a flop.
So when the walls are crumbling . . .

CHORUS:

> Yes?

BEN:

> Don't give up the ship.

CHORUS:

> No.

BEN:

> Learn how to laugh,
> Learn how to love,
> Learn how to live,
> That's my tip.
> When I hear the rumbling,

CHORUS:

> Yes?

BEN:

> Do I lose my grip?

CHORUS:

> No!

BEN:

> I have to laugh,
> I have to love,
> I have to live.
> That's my trip.

BEN AND CHORUS:

> When the wind is blowing,
> That's all the time to smile . . .

> *(They dance.)*

When the rent is owing,
Never lose your style . . .

(Ben dances nimbly and does some fancy work with a hat and cane, à la Fred Astaire.)

BEN:

Some get a boot
From shooting off cablegrams
Or buzzing bells
To summon the staff.
Some climbers get their kicks
From social politics.
Me, I like to live,
Me, I like to love,
Me, I like to . . .

(He forgets the lyric. He calls for it from the conductor, who barks it to him; Ben recovers his poise.)

Some break their asses
Passing their bar exams,
Lay out their lives
Like lines on a graph . . .
One day they're diplomats—
Well, bully and congrats!
Me, I like to live,
Me, I like to love,
Me, I . . .

(He goes completely blank. Then he sings, shouting desperately:)

Me, I like—me, I love—me.
I DON'T LOVE ME!

(The Chorus line keeps dancing. Ben turns, shouts at one Chorus Girl after another as the amplified voices of the offstage party guests get louder and louder:)

BEN: Look at me. I'm nothing. Can't you see it? I'm a fraud. It's all a trick. You couldn't love me. No one could. You'd be a fool to trust me. All I'll do is hurt you, tell you lies. Her zipper stuck and I kept saying: "Phyl, I love you . . . I love you . . ."

CHORUS: Success is swell And success is sweet, But every height has a drop. The less achievement The less defeat. What's the point of shovin' Your way to the top?

(The cacophony is all but deafening. Then sudden silence. All but Ben stand motionless. We can scarcely hear Ben as he screams:)

Phyllis!

(A flash of light and deafening sound as everything breaks apart and disassembles insanely. Bits and pieces of other songs shatter through. The Chorus line, although broken up, is still dancing, as if in a nightmare. The noise reaches a peak of madness before slowly starting to recede. Softer, softer . . . leaving Ben kneeling on the stage as a solitary ghostly Showgirl drifts by.)

(Cries out, shaken) Phyllis!

PHYLLIS: I'm here, Ben. I'm right here.

BEN: I need you, Phyl.

PHYLLIS: I know.

BEN: I've always been afraid of you. You see straight through me, I've always thought, It isn't possible: it can't be me she loves.

PHYLLIS *(Handing him his jacket)*: Come on, let's get our coats.

(They move to one side as Sally enters; Buddy follows.)

BUDDY: Hey, kid, it's me.

SALLY: I left the dishes in the sink. I left them there, I was in such a hurry and there is no Ben for me, not ever, anyplace.

BUDDY: There never was, and that's the truth.

SALLY *(Breaking down)*: I'm forty-nine years old, that's all I am. What am I going to do?

(Guests in overcoats and evening wraps begin to cross the stage, exiting.)

DEEDEE: You know what? We should do this every year.

SANDRA: Are you insane?

EMILY: There's still time for a nightcap.

SOLANGE: No, no, no. I need my beauty sleep.

HATTIE: I'll say you do.

SAM *(To Carlotta and Stella)*: Ladies? One for the road?

CARLOTTA: Why stop at one? The party's never over, not while I'm around. Right, Stella?

STELLA: Honey, you're an inspiration to me.

(They exit.)

HEIDI *(Gazing fondly at the theatre)*: Ah, Mitya, don't you hate to see it go?

WEISMANN: If nothing else, I know when things are over.

*(They exit as the two couples come together and awkwardly face each other.
Emerging from the shadows, the young selves approach their older counterparts.)*

BEN *(To Sally)*: There's no way I can make amends. I feel—
SALLY: Don't say it. I'm all right. *(To Phyllis)* You take good
    care of him.
PHYLLIS: I'll do my best.
BUDDY: So long, Ben.
BEN: Next time you're back in town—
BUDDY: Sure, sure. And if you're ever out in Phoenix—

(Silence. They have nothing left to say.
    The young selves watch as Ben and Phyllis, and Buddy
and Sally slowly exit.)

YOUNG BUDDY:
    Hey, up there . . .

YOUNG BEN:
    Way up there . . .

YOUNG BEN AND YOUNG BUDDY:
    Whaddaya say up there!

YOUNG SALLY: Hi . . .
YOUNG BEN: Girls . . .
YOUNG PHYLLIS: Ben . . .
YOUNG BUDDY: Sally . . .

(The door closes. The stage goes black.)

CURTAIN

JAMES GOLDMAN's career gave us distinguished and successful work in an unusual variety of fields. For the theatre, he wrote *The Lion in Winter*, *They Might Be Giants* (produced and directed by Joan Littlewood at Stratford East), *Blood, Sweat and Stanley Pool* (with his brother, William), the original *Follies* and the musical *A Family Affair*, for which he also wrote the lyrics (with John Kander). His other lyrics include ballads for his films: *Robin and Marian* and *The Lion in Winter* (music by John Barry).

He received an Academy Award and Best Screenplay Awards from the Writers Guilds of America and Great Britain for *The Lion in Winter*. His other films include *Nicholas and Alexandra*, *They Might Be Giants* and *White Nights*.

A novelist as well, Mr. Goldman's credits include *Waldorf, The Man from Greek and Roman*, *Myself As Witness* and *Fulton Country*.

For television, he wrote *Evening Primrose* (with Stephen Sondheim), *Oliver Twist*, *Anna Karenina* and the mini-series *Anastasia*.

He also authored many articles on food and wine, including his contribution to *Where to Eat in America*.

Mr. Goldman served on the councils of the Dramatists Guild and the Author's League of America from 1966 until his death in 1998.

STEPHEN SONDHEIM wrote the music and lyrics for *Passion* (1994), *Assassins* (1991), *Into the Woods* (1987), *Sunday in the Park with George* (1984), *Merrily We Roll Along* (1981), *Sweeney Todd* (1979), *Pacific Overtures* (1976), *The Frogs* (1974), *A Little Night Music* (1973), *Follies* (1971, revised in London, 1987 and in New York, 2001), *Company* (1970), *Anyone Can Whistle* (1964) and *A Funny Thing Happened on the Way to the Forum* (1962), as well as lyrics for *West Side Story* (1957), *Gypsy* (1959), *Do I Hear a Waltz?* (1965) and additional lyrics for *Candide* (1973). *Side by Side by Sondheim* (1976), *Marry Me a Little* (1981), *You're Gonna Love Tomorrow* (1983) and *Putting It Together* (1992, 2000) are anthologies of his work.

For film, he composed the scores of *Stavisky* (1974) and *Reds* (1981) and songs for *Dick Tracy* (Academy Award, 1990). He also wrote songs for the television production *Evening Primrose* (1966), co-authored the film *The Last of Sheila* (1973) and the play *Getting Away with Murder* (1996), and provided incidental music for the plays *The Girls of Summer* (1956), *Invitation to a March* (1961) and *Twigs* (1971).

He won Tony Awards for Best Score for a Musical for *Passion, Into the Woods, Sweeney Todd, A Little Night Music, Follies* (1971) and *Company*: all of these shows won the New York Drama Critics Circle Award, as did *Pacific Overtures* and *Sunday in the Park with George*, the latter also receiving the Pulitzer Prize for Drama (1985).

Mr. Sondheim was born in 1930 and raised in New York City. He graduated from Williams College, winning the Hutchinson Prize for Music Composition, after which he studied theory and composition with Milton Babbitt.

He is on the Council of the Dramatists Guild, the national association of playwrights, composers and lyricists, having served as its president from 1973 to 1981, and in 1983 was elected to the American Academy of Arts and Letters. In 1990 he was appointed the first Visiting Professor of Contemporary Theatre at Oxford University, and in 1993 was a recipient of the Kennedy Center Honors.